Learning the Basics
The Brainy Bunch Kids

The Complete Resource for Teaching Early Childhood Curriculum through Stories, Fun Activities, and Games

by
Becky White

illustrated by
Julie Anderson

Publisher
Key Education Publishing Company, LLC
Minneapolis, Minnesota 55431

www.keyeducationpublishing.com

CONGRATULATIONS ON YOUR PURCHASE OF A KEY EDUCATION PRODUCT!

The editors at Key Education are former teachers who bring experience, enthusiasm, and quality to each and every product. Thousands of teachers have looked to the staff at Key Education for new and innovative resources to make their work more enjoyable and rewarding. We are committed to developing educational materials that will assist teachers in building a strong and developmentally appropriate curriculum for young children.

PLAN FOR GREAT TEACHING EXPERIENCES WHEN YOU USE
EDUCATIONAL MATERIALS FROM KEY EDUCATION PUBLISHING COMPANY, LLC

ABC •123 •▲○■ • ABC •123 •▲○■ • ABC •123 •▲○■ • ABC •123 •▲○■ • ABC •123 •▲○■ • ABC •123 •▲○■ • ABC •123 •▲○■ • ABC

Credits

Author: Becky White
Publisher: Sherrill B. Flora
Creative Director: Annette Hollister-Papp
Inside Illustrations: Julie Anderson
Editors: Karen Seberg and Claude Chalk
Production: Key Education Staff

Key Education welcomes manuscripts and product ideas from teachers. For a copy of our submission guidelines, please send a self-addressed, stamped envelope to:

Key Education Publishing Company, LLC
Acquisitions Department
9601 Newton Avenue South
Minneapolis, Minnesota 55431

About the Author

Becky White has written more than 300 educational books for Key Education, Instructional Fair • T.S. Denison, Carson-Dellosa, Good Apple, Shining Star, The Education Center, Learning Works, and McGraw Hill. Her *Elementary Economics* (a six-book series for K–5 published by McGraw Hill), received *Learning* magazine's Teachers' Choice Gold Award for 2002. In 1980, Becky created a magazine called *Shining Star* for Good Apple Inc. and was its executive editor until 1993. Becky is a former elementary and middle school teacher and a graduate of California University at Long Beach. Becky is also the author of *Double Luck: Memoirs of a Chinese Orphan*, a true story of a boy's struggle to escape communist China and get to America. *Double Luck* was published by Holiday House in 2001 and won a Parents' Choice Gold Award for nonfiction.

Copyright Notice

Standard Book Number: 978-1-602680-18-0
The Brainy Bunch Kids—Learning the Basics
Copyright © 2009 by Key Education Publishing Company, LLC
Minneapolis, Minnesota 55431

Contents

Introduction
How to Use This Book 4
Directions for Assembling the Pullout Stories ...4

Chapter 1—All About Me
Teacher's Guide 5–8
Directions for
Reproducible Activity Pages.....................9–10
Pullout Story "Meet the Brainy Bunch" 11–22
Reproducible Activity Pages....................23–30

Chapter 2—Colors
Teacher's Guide 31–34
Directions for
Reproducible Activity Pages....................35–36
Pullout Story "The Mural" 37–48
Reproducible Activity Pages....................49–56

Chapter 3—Numbers
Teacher's Guide 57–60
Directions for
Reproducible Activity Pages....................61–62
Pullout Story
"The First School-Day Picnic" 63–74
Reproducible Activity Pages....................75–82

Chapter 4—Shapes
Teacher's Guide 83–86
Directions for
Reproducible Activity Pages....................87–88
Pullout Story "Show-and-Tell Shapes".....89–100
Reproducible Activity Pages................ 101–108

Chapter 5—Building Community
and Character
Teacher's Guide 109–112
Directions for
Reproducible Activity Pages................. 113–114
Pullout Story "The Library Fund-Raiser"... 115–126
Reproducible Activity Pages................. 127–134

Chapter 6—Prepositions
Teacher's Guide 135–138
Directions for
Reproducible Activity Pages................. 139–140
Pullout Story "The Hat Mystery" 141–152
Reproducible Activity Pages................. 153–160

Chapter 7—Alphabet
Teacher's Guide 161–164
Directions for
Reproducible Activity Pages................ 165–166
Pullout Story "The Name Game" 167–178
Reproducible Activity Pages................ 179–186

Chapter 8—Feelings
Teacher's Guide 187–189
Ruby Choral Reading............................. 190–192
Directions for
Reproducible Activity Pages.............. 193–194
Pullout Story "Rude Ruby".....................195–206
Reproducible Activity Pages.............. 207–212

Chapter 9—Transportation
Teacher's Guide 213–216
Directions for
Reproducible Activity Pages................ 217–218
Pullout Story
"The Transportation Song" 219–230
Reproducible Activity Pages................ 231–238

Chapter 10—The Farm
Teacher's Guide 239–243
Directions for
Reproducible Activity Pages........................244
Pullout Story
"Uncle Eual's Huge Blue Mule" 245–256
Reproducible Activity Pages................ 257–264

Chapter 11—Water
Teacher's Guide 265–268
Directions for
Reproducible Activity Pages....................269–270
Pullout Story "The Science Fair" 271–282
Reproducible Activity Pages................ 283–288

Chapter 12—Pets and Other Animals
Teacher's Guide 289–292
Directions for
Reproducible Activity Pages.................293–294
Pullout Story "NO PETS ALLOWED!" 295–306
Reproducible Activity Pages.................307–314

Brainy Bunch Puppet Patterns 315–318
Answer Key...319–320

Introduction

Come along on a series of exciting adventures with the Brainy Bunch kids! Your students will meet Eli, Jada, Yuuto, and Zoe—energetic and engaging friends starring in 12 colorful pullout storybooks that focus on important themes for early childhood education. In the first unit and story "All About Me," students will learn about themselves and each other along with the Brainy Bunch. Subsequent stories introduce and reinforce colors, numbers, shapes, position words, and the alphabet. Children will have the opportunity to explore feelings and learn about building community and character. The Brainy Bunch kids also share their experiences with pets, a trip to Uncle Eual's farm, and the excitement of entering a science fair. From fund-raising for new library books to solving the mystery of their teacher's missing hat, the Brainy Bunch will keep your students actively learning.

Each thematic unit is complete with ideas for learning centers and bulletin boards, field trips and outdoor adventures, and companion books to share. Small and large group activities highlight important skills such as listening, following directions, fine and gross motor movement, and critical thinking. There are ideas for music, crafts, discussion, drama, and games. Also included in each unit are six to eight reproducible student pages that offer fun comprehension activities, patterns, art projects, and much more.

As you and your students read and reread the stories in *The Brainy Bunch Kids—Learning the Basics*, you will surely agree with their teacher "that classes could be so much fun, teaching kids like these."

Directions for Assembling the Pullout Stories

1. Carefully remove the six full-color pages for each story. Trim the top edge of each page along the dashed line.

2. If you wish to create individual student books, make color copies of each page, both front and back. Assemble the copies in the correct order and staple each book's pages along its left edge.

3. To make a durable classroom book, cut two 9" x 11.5" (23 cm x 29 cm) pieces of card stock to make a cover. Or, cut a colorful file folder along the fold and trim off the tab.

4. Write the title of the book on the front cover and decorate it with colorful and appropriately themed artwork. You may also choose to make a color copy of the title page or other images in the book and attach them to the front cover.

5. Laminate or cover the pages and the book covers with clear contact paper for durability.

6. Hold each page so that you are looking at the odd-numbered side of the page. Align and punch two holes along the left edge of each.

7. Align and punch two holes in the left edge of each cover.

8. Assemble the book's pages in the correct order and add its front and back covers. Fasten the pages together with loose-leaf binder rings or brads or tie them with yarn.

9. Store the books in an easily accessible file folder box or on a shelf in your book center. Your students will return again and again to share adventures with the Brainy Bunch.

Chapter 1—All About Me
(Teacher's Guide)

Learning Center: Setting the Stage for the Pullout Story "Meet the Brainy Bunch"

Need: long table or empty shelves

Directions: Celebrate each student's individuality. Designate a table or shelf where children can exhibit their favorite objects. Take time each day to show and tell about the cherished objects. After sharing, place each item on the table with the owner's name. Examples for two weeks might include:

☐ **Monday**
favorite book

☐ **Tuesday**
favorite stuffed animal or toy

☐ **Wednesday**
favorite vehicle (picture/photo/drawing)

☐ **Thursday**
favorite food (picture/photo/drawing)

☐ **Friday**
favorite person (photo/drawing)

☐ **Monday**
sample of hobby or collection

☐ **Tuesday**
favorite article of clothing

☐ **Wednesday**
favorite animal (drawing)

☐ **Thursday**
favorite board or sports game

☐ **Friday**
favorite flower or plant (real/photo)

Bulletin Board: All About Me

Need: bulletin board, roll of white paper, black construction paper, 4" to 6" (10 cm to 15 cm) letter patterns, scissors, stapler or tape

Getting Ready: Cover a bulletin board or wall with white paper. Trace letter patterns on black paper and cut them out to make the title. Center the title at the top of the board.

Directions: A bulletin board to introduce individuals might become a yearlong project with each student getting a full week's use of the board. The "All About Me" board should include a collage of baby photos, family photos, mementos, awards such as ribbons, and descriptive pictures and large words cut from magazines. Encourage parents to help their child gather items for the board, come to class to assemble the board on Monday morning, and return on Friday to take it down. The first board might be all about you.

Field Trip Ideas: It's My Spot!

Any of the following excursions will celebrate individual student preferences.

☐ Visit a student's home and view her pets, family, yard, toys, bedroom, etc.

☐ Visit a student's parent's workplace, for example, a doctor's office, dental office, or store, and encourage the student to tell about his parent's work.

☐ Visit a student's favorite spot such as a park, zoo, or playground.

Presenting the Pullout Story: "Meet the Brainy Bunch"

Need: "Meet the Brainy Bunch" pullout story (pages 11–22); Brainy Bunch Puppet Patterns reproducibles (pages 315–318); flannel board; card stock; scissors; felt, flannel, sandpaper, pellon, or the loop side of hook-and-loop tape

Getting Ready: Before sharing the story, mount the Brainy Bunch puppets (pages 315–318) on card stock and cut them out. Laminate them for durability. Then, attach small pieces of felt or other material to the back of each character.

Directions: As you read the description of each child in the pullout story, display the appropriate puppet.

Discussion: How Are We Alike?

Directions: To reinforce the Brainy Bunch as friendly learning aids, follow the reading of the story with a discussion linking these four children with your students.

1. Which of the Brainies are you most like? Why do you say so?
2. Yuuto speaks two languages. What are they? Eli speaks two languages, too. What are they? Are you bilingual? What other language do you speak? (Take time to let students address the class in other languages.)
3. Yuuto plays the violin. Do you play a musical instrument? Which one?
4. Jada likes to write books. Do you like to write stories or books? Tell about one.
5. Eli loves sports. Are you a sports fan? Which sports do you like best?
6. Zoe said that at first she was afraid to stand up and talk. Are you sometimes afraid to talk in class?
7. Zoe lives with Grandma. Do you live with someone other than your mom or dad? Who?
8. Zoe said she is an only child. Are you an only child? How many children are in your family? Do you have brothers or sisters or both?
9. So far, what do you like best about each of the Brainies?

Companion Book: *I Am Me*

"I am positively absolutely altogether no one else but me."

Need: *I Am Me* by Karla Kuskin (Simon & Schuster Books for Young Readers)

Directions: The heroine has her mother's eyes, her father's nose, and Aunt Jen's funny little toes. Her eyebrows are like her grandma Ann's; her smile is like her aunt Grace's. This boldly illustrated book describes a little girl who resembles many of her relatives. After sharing the book, ask students to name a physical trait that they inherited. Then, have students draw self-portraits to take home and, with help from parents, label family traits.

Other Good Books to Share:
- ❑ *My Friend* by Beatrice Alemagna (North-South Books)
- ❑ *My Mom* by Anthony Browne (Farrar, Straus and Giroux)
- ❑ *Will You Take Care of Me?* by Margaret Park Bridges (Morrow Junior Books)

Drama: Let's Be the Brainies

Need: The Brainies reproducible (page 29) for each group of four students

Directions: Begin by dividing the class into groups of four—preferably two girls and two boys. Pass out page 29 to use as scripts. Have students decide as a group which Brainy each student will be. Help students memorize their lines. Scripts may also be taken home and rehearsed with parents. After each student has learned the appropriate lines, groups may take turns performing the story. An aid, an older student, or you should read the first three verses in the pullout story (pages 11–13) and the last verse (page 22) for each group.

Comprehension Activities: Make It True

Directions: Reread the story (pages 11–22). Then, tell students that you will make statements about the Brainies. If they think the statement is true, they should give a thumbs-up. Thumbs-down means the statement is false. After each thumbs-down, ask students to change the statement to make it true.

1. Yuuto is a sports fan. *(False—Eli is a sports fan.)*
2. Zoe lives with lots of brothers and sisters. *(False—Zoe lives with Grandma.)*
3. Jada writes books as a hobby. *(This statement is true.)*
4. Eli said he was afraid to talk to the class. *(False—Zoe was afraid to talk to the class.)*
5. Eli plays the violin. *(False—Yuuto plays the violin.)*
6. Jada's mother teaches violin. *(False—Yuuto's mother teaches violin.)*
7. Yuuto plays the flute. *(False—Yuuto plays the violin.)*
8. Zoe likes to read mystery stories every night. *(This statement is true.)*
9. Jada is the Brainy who speaks Japanese. *(False—Yuuto is the Brainy who speaks Japanese.)*
10. Zoe said she speaks Spanish. *(False—Eli said he speaks Spanish.)*
11. Zoe said she likes to skip rope and dance. *(This statement is true.)*
12. Grandma taught Eli how to read. *(False—Grandma taught Zoe how to read.)*

Language: Guess Who

Need: All About Me reproducible (page 24)

Getting Ready: Have each student take home page 24 and ask a parent to help fill it out.

Directions: Back in class, collect the fact sheets. In large group, randomly read facts from one student's sheet. *Examples:* This person has a brother named Mark. He lives on High Street. His favorite color is purple. Then, have the class take turns guessing who is being described. Keep giving facts until someone correctly identifies the mystery student.

Discussion: Meet One Another

Need: completed All About Me fact sheets (page 24)

Directions: Ask a student to come forward. Read three interesting facts from her All About Me fact sheet. *Examples:* Emily's favorite color is green. She has two sisters. Her goal is to be an astronaut. Then, ask students to guess one of the other responses. *Example:* What do you think Emily's favorite animal is? When someone guesses correctly, the student standing chooses the next student to come forward.

Following Directions: Drawing the Brainies

Need: paper, crayons

Directions: Have students listen and follow directions for drawing pictures.

1. Draw Eli's baseball.
2. Draw Jada's pencil.
3. Draw Zoe's jump rope.
4. Draw Yuuto's sheet of music.
5. Draw your favorite musical instrument.
6. Draw a book.
7. Draw a flower.
8. Color your pictures any colors you choose.

Music: You Are Special

Getting Ready: To hear and sing some very special self-concept songs, visit Mr. Rogers' Neighborhood. Go online to http://pbskids.org/rogers/songlist/ to hear Fred Rogers sing all of these uplifting hits.

"You Are Special"   "Everybody's Fancy"   "I'm Still Myself Inside"
"It's You I Like"   "You're Growing"   "I'm Proud of You"

Directions: Build positive self-images by teaching students these six songs and singing them again and again.

More of Fred Rogers's songs will be featured in Chapter 5—Building Community and Character and in Chapter 8—Feelings.

Critical Thinking: Which Brainy Might . . .

Directions: Gather students on the floor around you. Reread "Meet the Brainy Bunch." Then, have students use story clues to draw conclusions. Encourage a variety of creative answers.

1. Which of the Brainies do you think might dream of someday becoming a famous musician? *(Yuuto)*
2. Which of the Brainies do you think might be able to count to 10 in Spanish? *(Eli)*
3. Which of the Brainies do you think might be the shyest? *(Zoe)*
4. Which of the Brainies do you think might have lots of energy? Why? *(Zoe or Eli)*
5. Which of the Brainies do you think might dream of becoming a famous mystery writer? *(Jada or Zoe)*
6. Which of the Brainies do you think might hope to play professional sports someday? *(Eli)*
7. Which of the Brainies do you think can read? *(Eli, Jada, or Zoe)*
8. Which of the Brainies do you think can read music? *(Yuuto)*
9. Which of the Brainies do you think might dream of becoming a ballerina? *(Zoe)*
10. Which of the Brainies do you think might be the friendliest? *(Jada)*

Imagination: Playing with the Brainy Bunch

Need: a classical music CD and player

Directions: Invite students to lie back and relax. Instruct them to close their eyes and listen carefully to try to see with their imaginations what you will describe. Play quiet background music. To give students time to use their visual memories and imaginations, pause at least 20 seconds after each description.

1. It is a sunny day. You are sitting in the grass with friends listening to Yuuto play his violin. (pause)
2. You are sitting in the bleachers watching Eli play baseball. He is up to bat. He hits the ball hard, and it goes over the fence. The crowd goes wild. (pause)
3. You are on the phone with Jada. She is reading one of her stories to you. Listen carefully. (pause)
4. You are in an auditorium. Zoe is dancing on the stage. Can you see her? (pause)
5. You are on the playground. Zoe and Eli ask you to come and play dodgeball with them. (pause)
6. It is raining. You and Yuuto are sitting on his porch, watching gutters fill up with rain. (pause)
7. You and Jada are sitting under a tree eating your lunches. What are you eating? (pause)
8. It is snowing. You and all of the Brainies are building a snowman. (pause)
9. You are camping with your favorite Brainy. You are roasting hot dogs and marshmallows. (pause)

Follow-Up: Hold a discussion. Say, "Pretend it is your birthday. All four of the Brainies are at your party." Ask, "What do you think each of the Brainies would give you for a present?" Take turns naming things and have students say why they think each Brainy would choose that gift.

Directions for Reproducible Activity Pages

Fine Motor: My Name—Page 23

Need: My Name reproducible (page 23), pencils

Directions: Remind students that Yuuto said, "My name is Japanese." Have students take turns telling their names. As you print each name on the board, ask, "How was your name chosen?" Add the information beside each name. Parents may also supply this information at the bottom of page 23. If possible, use a computer to discover the meanings of several of the children's names. There are a variety of online sites that provide information about the origin and meanings of names. One easy-to-use site is: http://www.babynamesworld.com/. Send page 23 home with students.

Follow-Up: When pages have been completed and returned, share the information in large group about how students' names were chosen and their meanings.

Connecting with Family: All About Me—Page 24

Need: All About Me reproducible (page 24)

Directions: Have each student take home page 24 and ask a parent or another adult to help fill it out. There are many ways to use the completed page. (See two game ideas on page 7: Guess Who and Meet One Another.) Pair students and have them share and compare some of the interesting facts on their sheets.

Follow-Up: Allow time for each pair of students to introduce each other and tell two to four interesting things that were learned.

Craft: That's Me!—Page 25

Need: That's Me! reproducible (page 25), white sturdy paper, old magazines, scissors, glue sticks, crayons, markers

Getting Ready: Reproduce page 25 on white sturdy paper.

Directions: Have each student make a collage about himself. Encourage students to think about the image that they want to create before they begin. They might include self-portraits and pictures of their favorites (food, animals, etc.) plus photocopies of photos of themselves and family members. They can also cut and paste self-descriptive words from magazines.

Follow-Up: When collages are completed, share them in large group. Then, display them on a bulletin board.

Connecting with Family: I Have Roots!—Page 26

Need: I Have Roots! reproducible (page 26), colorful sturdy paper

Getting Ready: Reproduce the family tree on page 26 on colorful paper.

Directions: There are no written directions on this page, so explain that students will complete the page with adult help. Students may record names or cut and paste photocopies of photos on the branches.

Follow-Up: Back in class, break into small groups. Have students share their family trees with each other. Display all of the family trees on a bulletin board entitled "We Have Roots."

Directions for Reproducible Activity Pages, CONTINUED

Story Recall: Matching—Page 27

Need: Matching reproducible (page 27), scissors, glue sticks, crayons

Directions: Have students cut out the pictures at the bottom of the page. Match the objects and Brainies by cutting apart and gluing the pictures in the appropriate boxes. Allow time for students to color the pictures.

Visual Memory: What's Missing?—Page 28

Need: What's Missing? reproducible (page 28), pencils, crayons

Directions: Explain that students should compare the two pictures to find what is missing in the bottom picture. Then, ask students to draw the 11 missing things so that the pictures are alike. Allow time for students to color the pictures to make them identical.

Listening Skills: Brainy Booklet—Page 29

Need: The Brainies reproducible (page 29), pencils, crayons

Directions: Pass out page 29. Using the flannel board puppets (patterns on pages 315–318 and directions on page 6), reread the story, "Meet the Brainy Bunch" (pages 11–22). Invite students to follow along on their sheets as you read the two verses about each of the Brainies. Next, have students draw and color a picture of the appropriate Brainy in each box.

Outdoor Adventure: BINGO—Page 30

Need: BINGO reproducible (page 30), pencils

Getting Ready: To encourage students to meet children who are not in their class, prepare special BINGO cards.

1. Reproduce one BINGO card (page 30) and use it to create a master card for this activity.
2. Under *B*, draw an eye.
3. Under *I*, draw a musical note.
4. Under *N*, print *Name*.
5. Under *G*, print *Game*.
6. Under *O*, print *Orange*.
7. Reproduce this special BINGO card for each student.

Directions: Before leaving for five separate recesses, read one of the instructions below. During the recess, students should find children to autograph the appropriate spaces.

Monday: Find five people with blue eyes to autograph a space under *B*.

Tuesday: Find five people who play a musical instrument to autograph a space under *I*.

Wednesday: Find four people whose names begin with the letter *N* to autograph a space under *N*.

Thursday: Find five people who like to play games or sports to autograph a space under *G*.

Friday: Find five people whose favorite fruit or color is orange to autograph a space under *O*.

Chapter 1—All About Me

Meet the Brainy Bunch

The first day of school,

With new books
on the shelves,

The teacher told her students,

"Tell us about yourselves."

KE-804011 © Key Education

"In this class, we each will share. And, to get you started,
Some things with all the rest. Tell what you know best."

Welcome to School

Twenty students spoke that day,

But four of them stood out.

These were extra special;

Of this, she had no doubt.

KE-804011 © Key Education

The Brainy Bunch Kids—Learning the Basics

The first to stand was Yuuto.

"My name is Japanese. Although I speak it in my home,

With English, I'm at ease."

KE-804011 © Key Education

14

"My mother teaches violin.
I practice all I can.
So, I'll be playing concerts
When I become a man."

The next to speak was Jada. "I'm pleased to be here with you. She flashed a friendly grin. I know we'll all be friends."

"I guess my hobby's writing books.
I started at age four.

Now, I'm working on my sixth,
Called *Monster at My Door*."

The Brainy Bunch Kids—Learning the Basics

Eli stood up front and said,
"Buenos dias and good day."

He jerked his thumb into the air,
"There's much that I could say."

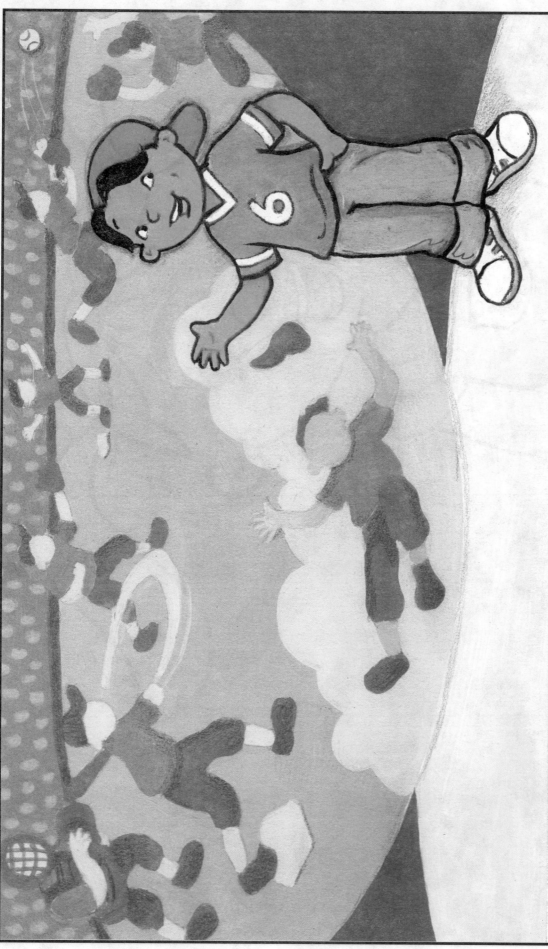

"Baseball, soccer, football, too,   I know all of the players

The sports page starts my day.   And how much they're paid."

The Brainy Bunch Kids—Learning the Basics

Zoe said, "I was afraid
To stand up front and talk.

But, now that I am finally here,
I'm not scared at all."

KE-804011 © Key Education

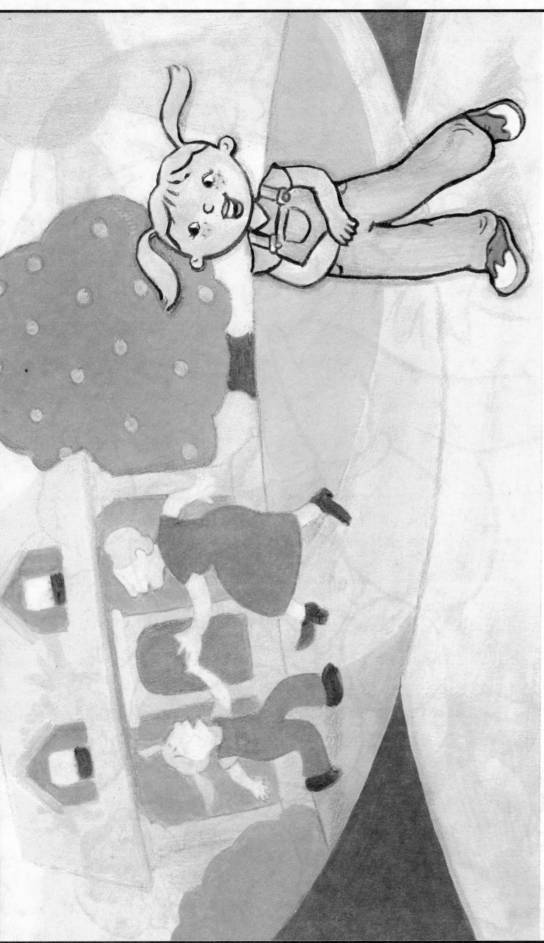

"I live alone with Grandma.
She taught me how to write.

I love to dance, skip rope, and read
Mysteries every night."

Their teacher thought, a brainy bunch. That classes could be so much fun, She could plainly see Teaching kids like these.

My Name

Directions: Ask an adult to help you by printing your name on the top line. Then, copy it three times below.

I Can Print My Name

To the Parent: Share with your child how your child's name was chosen and write it below. Then, together find out the meaning of your child's name. One especially easy-to-use online site is http://www.babynamesworld.com/.

How my name was chosen: _____

_____

My name means:_____

Please return this completed page by:_____

⸲★℮~★ All About Me ★~℮★⸲

Directions: Ask your parent or another adult to fill out this page with you. Bring it back to school tomorrow.

Name _____

Age _____ Birthday _____

Address _____

Phone_____ E-mail Address _____

Brothers (names and ages) _____

Sisters (names and ages) _____

Best Friend(s)_____

Pets (kinds and names) _____

Hobbies_____

Favorite Animal _____

Favorite Color _____

Favorite Food _____

Favorite Number _____

Favorite Subject _____

Favorite Song or Recording_____

Favorite TV Program _____

Favorite Book _____

Favorite Person _____

Favorite Magazine_____

Favorite Sport or Game_____

Things That Bug Me _____

Secret Wish_____

Things I Hate to Do _____

What I Want to Do When I Grow Up _____

Language(s) I Speak_____

Favorite Place to Go _____

Farthest Away Place I Have Been _____

Place I Most Want to Visit _____

Name _____   Date _____

That's Me!

Directions: Make a collage all about you. Draw pictures of yourself and your favorites. Cut and paste words from magazines that describe you.

Name _____   **Date** _____

(See directions on page 9.)

I Have Roots!

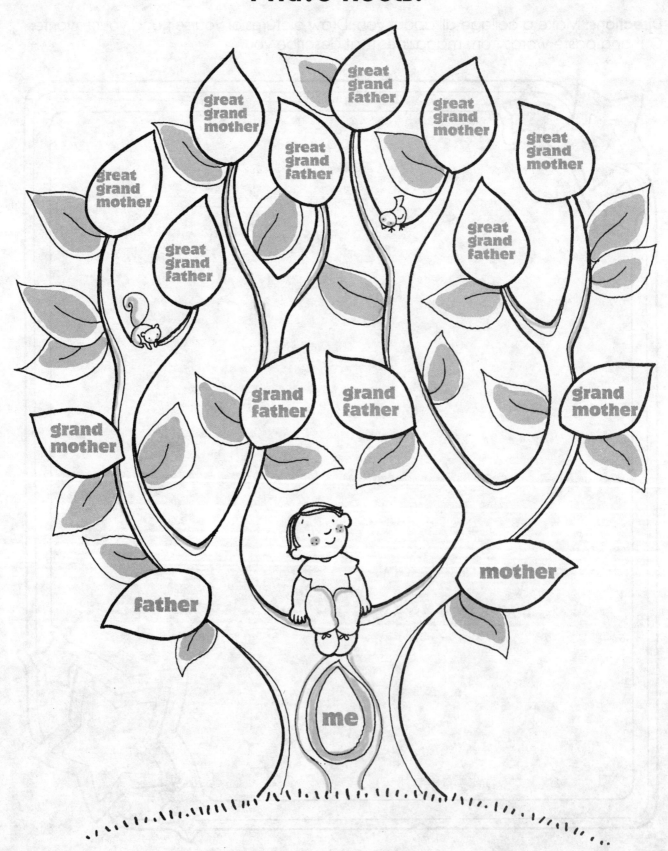

Name _____   **Date** _____

Matching

Directions: Cut out the pictures below on the dashed lines. Match each object with its owner. Glue it in the correct box. Color the pictures.

Name _____   Date _____

What's Missing?

Directions: Compare the two pictures of the Brainy Bunch. Find 11 things that are missing in the bottom picture. Draw the 11 missing things. Color the pictures the same.

(See directions on pages 7 and 10.)

The Brainies

The first to stand was Yuuto.
"My name is Japanese.
Although I speak it in my home,
With English, I'm at ease."

"My mother teaches violin.
I practice all I can.
So, I'll be playing concerts
When I become a man."

The next to speak was Jada.
She flashed a friendly grin.
"I'm pleased to be here with you.
I know we'll all be friends."

"I guess my hobby's writing books.
I started at age four.
Now, I'm working on my sixth,
Called *Monster at My Door*."

Eli stood up front and said,
"Buenos dias and good day."
He jerked his thumb into the air,
"There's much that I could say."

"Baseball, soccer, football, too,
The sports page starts my day.
I know all of the players
And how much they're paid."

Zoe said, "I was afraid
To stand up front and talk.
But, now that I am finally here,
I'm not scared at all."

"I live alone with Grandma.
She taught me how to write.
I love to dance, skip rope, and read
Mysteries every night."

(See directions on pages 10, 34, 60, and 166.)

B	I	N	G	O
		free		

Chapter 2—Colors
(Teacher's Guide)

Learning Center: Setting the Stage for the Pullout Story "The Mural"

Need: long table(s), bulletin board for displaying Monet prints

Directions: Set up a learning center where students may explore and celebrate colors. As a backdrop for the learning center, have students create a Monets at Work mural (page 32).The center might include:

- ☐ companion picture book *Linnea in Monet's Garden* by Christina Bjork (R. & S. Books) and other good books to share listed below
- ☐ Monet prints, especially several versions of *The Japanese Bridge* or *Water Lilies*, *Poppy Field*, etc.
- ☐ pictures of colorful gardens or blooming flowers
- ☐ pictures of colorful foods
- ☐ several jumbo boxes of crayons and cupcake tins for sorting hues (blues, reds, etc.)
- ☐ colorful 6"x6" (15 cm x 15 cm) construction paper cards, each labeled with the appropriate color word
- ☐ pots of blooming flowers (artificial or real) in primary and secondary colors
- ☐ seed and flower catalogs for cutting and pasting
- ☐ watercolor paints, watercolor paper, and brushes for mixing colors

Companion Book: *Linnea in Monet's Garden*

"It was then I noticed that the lilies were nothing but blobs and blotches of paint. But when I stepped away again, they turned into real water lilies floating in a pond—magic!"

Need: *Linnea in Monet's Garden* by Christina Bjork (R. & S. Books)

Directions: Before reading the Brainy Bunch story, "The Mural," share the companion book, *Linnea in Monet's Garden*. Or, show the video with the same title, which is based on the book (First Run Features, 1993). If sharing the book, which is a bit long, divide the presentation into several readings. Then, after you have read pages 14 and 15 "At the Museum," it is the perfect time to share the Brainy Bunch story, "The Mural."

Other Good Books to Share:

- ☐ *Planting a Rainbow* by Lois Ehlert (Harcourt Brace Jovanovich)
- ☐ *Spicy Hot Colors: Colores Picantes* by Sherry Shahan (August House LittleFolk)

Presenting the Pullout Story: "The Mural"

Need: "The Mural" story (pages 37–48), watercolor paints, water, brush, large sheet of watercolor paper, easel

Directions: For a dramatic presentation, use these step-by-step directions for painting with watercolors as you tell the Brainy Bunch story.

page 38—Paint most of the paper blue, leaving space on the right for the sun.

page 39—Paint red over the blue sky to create purple streaks.

page 40—Along the bottom of the page, paint green stems and grass.

page 41—Paint pink blooms on the green stems.

page 42—Paint a perfectly round yellow sun on the right.

page 43—Paint orange over the yellow sun and make it less rounded.

page 44—Paint a few brown Vs in the sky.

pages 45 through 47—Finish reading the story as you point to your painting.

page 48—Move the easel across the room so that students may view it from farther away.

Follow-Up: Hold a discussion about your painting. See Art Critics on page 32.

Discussion: Art Critics

Directions: Discuss your painting and the Brainies' painting with the following questions.
1. How do you like my painting up close? From far away? Which is better?
2. Have you ever done something and thought it was not very good, but later gone back and realized that it was quite good after all?
3. Do you think that the Brainy Bunch enjoyed painting the mural? Why or why not?
4. Which Brainy do you think enjoyed the experience the most? Why?
5. Which painter seemed the most serious about the mural? Why do you say so?
6. Which Brainy was willing to express disappointment about the mural?
7. Do you think the Brainy Bunch cooperated while performing the task?
8. Do you think the Brainies had a plan before they began?

Follow-Up: If available, have students look at a Monet print up close and then step back and view it again.

Bulletin Board: Monets at Work

Need: bulletin board; roll of white paper; black construction paper; 4" to 6" (10 cm to 15 cm) letter patterns; scissors; stapler or tape; pencils; red, blue, and yellow watercolor paints; water; brushes

Getting Ready: Cover a bulletin board or wall with white paper. Trace letter patterns on black paper and cut them out to make the title. Center the title at the top of the board.

Directions: Celebrate the Brainy Bunch story by having students paint a mural of a garden, bridge, park, or any outdoor scene. As they use the primary colors, encourage students to paint layers of primary colors to create the secondary colors. When the mural is finished, first look at it up close and then view it from a distance.

Follow-Up: Hold a discussion about the mural.
1. What do you like best about the mural?
2. What part did you paint? Did you enjoy cooperating and doing your part?
3. Which do you like better—working with others or working by yourself?
4. What is the best thing about working with others? By yourself?
5. Monet painted the same scene more than once. Each time the paintings looked different. If the class painted the mural again tomorrow, would it be exactly the same? Why or why not?

Imagination: Colorful Minds

Need: a classical music CD and player

Directions: Invite students to lie back and relax. Instruct them to close their eyes and listen carefully to try to see with their imaginations the things you will describe. Play quiet background music. To give students time to use their visual memories and imaginations, pause at least 20 seconds after each description.

1. black sky sparkling with stars (pause)
2. huge, orange sun in a blue sky (pause)
3. purple and red sky at sunset (pause)
4. pink flowers with green leaves (pause)
5. yellow full moon (pause)
6. red brick wall with brown spots (pause)
7. chocolate ice cream cone (pause)
8. shimmering, wet, silver seashells (pause)
9. red apples in a blue bowl (pause)
10. orange bird flapping brown wings (pause)
11. blue swirls, sparking like fireworks (pause)
12. pink and white squiggles in grass (pause)
13. red wall turning to pink . . . to orange (pause)
14. blue sky fading to gray and rain begins (pause)
15. green blotches turning to orange . . . to pink . . . to red (pause)
16. dancing pink polka dots (pause)
17. red swirls that explode with fire (pause)
18. orange-red blobs floating on the ocean (pause)
19. yellow snails on a pink sidewalk (pause)
20. brown spotted cow in green grass (pause)

Visual Memory: Pink Dogs?

Directions: Tell students to listen as you name an object and a color. If the object is that color, they should give a thumbs-up. Showing a thumbs-down means the object is *never* that color. After playing the game awhile, pair students and let partners take turns challenging each other with sets of objects and colors.

1. pink dogs (What colors are dogs? Can you name a pink animal?)
2. yellow apples (What other colors are apples?)
3. purple jam (What flavor of jam is purple?)
4. yellow ketchup (What color is ketchup? What hot dog topping is yellow?)
5. green pig (What colors are pigs? Which animals come in shades of green?)
6. pink lemonade (What other drinks are pink?)
7. red rabbits (What colors are rabbits? Have you ever seen a red bird?)
8. white jelly beans (What color jelly bean is your favorite flavor?)
9. blue coconut flakes (What color are coconut flakes? Can you name another white food?)
10. black snow (What color is snow? Name something else you might see in the sky that is white.)
11. white moth (Name some butterfly colors.)
12. an all orange rainbow (Name a color found in a rainbow.)

Critical Thinking: Name It

Directions: Gather students on the floor around you. Explain that you will give three clues about a common object. When they think they know what you are describing, students should raise their hands. After giving all three of the clues for an object, ask someone with a raised hand to name it. Often, there will be more than one correct answer. Encourage a variety of answers.

	Clue 1	Clue 2	Clue 3
1.	a fruit	crunchy	sometimes red (*apple*)
2.	an animal that hops	lives in water	green (*frog*)
3.	a dessert	birthday treat	iced in different colors (*cake*)
4.	an insect	works hard, never sleeps	often black (*ant*)
5.	made with lemons	a drink	sometimes pink (*lemonade*)
6.	a fruit	cannot eat the skin	yellow (*banana*)
7.	a small cake	wrapped in paper	brown (*chocolate cupcake*)
8.	very light and very sweet	sold at fairs	often pink (*cotton candy*)
9.	seen in the sky	follows a rain	many colors (*rainbow*)
10.	a fruit	comes in bunches	green, purple, or red (*grapes*)

Outdoor Adventure: I Spy

Getting Ready: Go outside and invite students to sit on the grass or benches.
How to Play: The first player chooses an object in the area and names the color. *Example:* "I spy something red." Others take turns guessing what the chosen object is. The student who guesses correctly chooses the next object.

Field Trip Ideas: Our Colorful Community

Any of the following excursions will provide vivid colors to recognize and discuss.
- Visit an art museum to view paintings up close and from far away.
- Visit a nursery or flower market and name the colors of blooming plants.
- Visit an art studio and talk to an artist about how she uses colors.
- Visit a paint/wallpaper store and look at paint chips and wallpaper samples.

Music: Sing the Colors

Need: scissors; colorful construction paper (blue, orange, yellow, red, green, purple, brown, pink, and gray); stapler; pointer

Directions: Cut out a circle of each color of construction paper. Attach the circles to the board in the order listed. As you sing the song below to the tune of "Clementine," use a pointer to indicate which color to sing next. For more fun, make the sock puppets (see below) and have students use them as they sing the song again.

Blue and orange,   Lovely colors in my crayon box.
Yellow, red, and green,   I use colors every day.
Purple, brown, and pink and gray.

Craft: Sock Puppets

Need: socks in a variety of colors (red, orange, yellow, green, blue, purple, brown, pink, and gray); scissors; glue; decorations for making puppet features (beads, felt, feathers, buttons, yarn, etc.)

Directions: Give each student a sock. Help students put the socks on their nondominant hands. Have each student push the sock in between the thumb and the rest of the hand to make a mouth. Attach a felt tongue by putting glue on the base of the tongue and placing it inside the puppet's mouth where the thumb and index finger meet. To complete the puppets' faces, students may use glue to attach beads, felt cutouts, feathers, buttons, etc.

Surprise Activity: Colorful Week

Directions: Just for fun, encourage all students to wear a certain color on each day for one week. *Examples:*

Monday—red   **Wednesday**—yellow   **Friday**—student's favorite color
Tuesday—blue   **Thursday**—green

Craft: A Mixer

Need: red, yellow, and blue tempera paint; plastic bowls; brushes; poster board

Directions: Divide students into small groups. Give each group bowls of paint in the primary colors, brushes, and a piece of poster board. Challenge each group to cooperate to create a sign that shows mixing of the primary colors to make the secondary colors. Share completed posters in large group.

Game: Color BINGO

Need: BINGO reproducible (page 30); red, orange, yellow, green, blue, purple, pink, and brown crayons; sturdy paper

Getting Ready:
1. Reproduce the BINGO card on page 30 for each student.
2. Cut the sturdy paper into 1.5" x 1.5" (4 cm x 4 cm) paper chips to cover the BINGO squares. Give 25 chips to each student.
3. Have students use all of the colors listed above to randomly color the squares on their cards but without repeating the same color in any column under a letter.

How to Play: Randomly call a letter and color, for example, B—yellow. Students will use paper chips to cover the corresponding squares on their cards. The first player to cover five in a row horizontally, vertically, or diagonally calls "BINGO!" and wins the game.

Directions for Reproducible Activity Pages

Discussion: My Color Wheel—Page 49

Need: My Color Wheel reproducible (page 49); pencils; red, yellow, and blue crayons

Directions: Reread the story, "The Mural." Then, encourage students to identify the primary and secondary colors with these discussion questions:

1. What are the three primary colors? (List them on the board.)
2. What happened in the story when Zoe painted red over Eli's blue sky?
3. What happened when Zoe painted orange over Yuuto's yellow sun?
4. Which two colors make orange? Purple? Green?
5. What happened when Zoe mixed white and red?
6. What do you think might happen if you mixed a drop of black with red?

Pass out page 49 and read the directions together. Help students complete the color wheels.

Language: Favorite Colors Graph—Page 50

Need: Favorite Colors Graph reproducible (page 50), pencils, crayons

Directions: On the board, draw a graph like the worksheet on page 50. Have students take turns naming their favorite colors. Use the initials of students' first and last names to record the information on the graph working from bottom to top. Emphasize to students that choosing different colors than their friends choose is good, too. Pass out page 50. Explain that students should have classmates sign their names in the boxes, each student signing above his favorite color. Remind them to work from the bottom to the top, adding names in the bottom boxes first. Then, to complete their graphs, have students color each box that has a name written in it.

Follow-Up: When the graphs are finished, meet as a large group to compare them. Are the graph results similar to the graph created on the board?

Following Directions: Colorful Picnic—Page 51

Need: Colorful Picnic reproducible (page 51), pencils, crayons

Directions: Pass out page 51. Explain that students should listen carefully and color the picture according to your directions. Allow plenty of time for coloring.

1. Look for the grape-jam sandwich. Color the jam purple. Don't color the bread.
2. Find the wedge of cheese. Color it yellow.
3. Look for the basket of blueberries. Color the berries blue. Color the basket yellow.
4. Find the apple. Color it red.
5. Find the pear. Color it yellow.
6. Do you see the pickle? Color it green.
7. Color the carrot orange and the carrot top green.
8. The cupcake is chocolate. Color it brown.
9. Find the hot dog in a bun. Color the hot dog red and the mustard yellow.
10. See the ants? Color them black.
11. Color the watermelon rind green, the watermelon red, and the seeds black.

Outdoor Adventure: My Colorful Hike—Page 52

Need: My Colorful Hike (page 52), pencils, crayons

Directions: Pass out page 52. Then, take students on a hike around the school grounds or to a nearby park or woods. Have students look for things in nature that are the 10 colors listed on their worksheets (plus favorite color and any color) and illustrate each one.

Follow-Up: Back in the classroom, have students color their drawings.

Directions for Reproducible Activity Pages, CONTINUED

Snack: Colorful Snacks—Page 53

Need: Colorful Snacks reproducible (page 53), pencils, crayons, scissors, glue sticks

Directions: Begin by discussing students' favorite foods and the foods' colors.

1. What is your favorite flavor of cupcake? What color is that flavor?
2. What flavor is your favorite frozen juice bar? What color is that flavor?
3. What flavor is your favorite ice cream bar? What color is that flavor?
4. What is your favorite pie? What color is that kind of pie?
5. What color is popcorn? What color might chocolate-covered popcorn be?
6. What color are grapes? Which do you like best: green, purple, or red grapes?
7 What color are peaches? Strawberries?
8. What color might coconut ice cream be?

Pass out page 53. Read aloud the color word in each box. Explain that students will cut out the pictures of snacks and glue a picture in each box. Remind students that some foods can be more than one color. Allow time for students to color the pictures.

Follow-Up: When the pages are completed, meet as a large group and have students name the flavors of foods. End the lesson with a colorful treat such as strawberries, grapes, frozen juice bars, etc.

Fine Motor: I Can Print Color Words—Page 54

Need: I Can Print Color Words reproducible (page 54), pencils, crayons

Directions: Pass out page 54. Read aloud the directions. Make sure students understand that first they will use the appropriate color of crayon to trace each word. Then, they will print each word with a pencil.

Story Recall: Who Did What?—Page 55

Need: Who Did What? reproducible (page 55), pencils, crayons

Directions: Pass out page 55 and review the name of each of the Brainy Bunch kids. Once again, read aloud the story "The Mural." Then, ask the questions on page 55 as students follow along. Have students answer each question by circling the correct Brainy picture or pictures using the same color of crayon as the color featured in the question. Any color may be used to answer questions 10–12.

Follow-Up: After students have completed the worksheets, meet in large group. Again, read the story. Have students raise their hands when they hear an answer to one of the questions. Then, discuss the question and its answer.

Surprise Activity: By the Seashore—Page 56

Need: By the Seashore reproducible (page 56), watercolor paints, brushes, paper cups of water, newspaper for work surface, pencils

Directions: Pass out page 56. Help students color code the numbers by coloring the boxes as indicated. Have students work independently to complete the paintings.

Follow-Up: Take paints, brushes, and watercolor paper outside. Allow time for students to watercolor outdoor scenes.

The Mural

Their teacher asked the
Brainy Bunch
To paint a mural in the hall.

"I've a little hunch, when we
break for lunch,
We'll be cheered by it on the wall."

37

The four met in a day or two
With paints and supplies
stacked high.

Before the rest knew, Eli grabbed
the blue,
And he brushed on a wide
piece of sky.

KE-804011 © Key Education

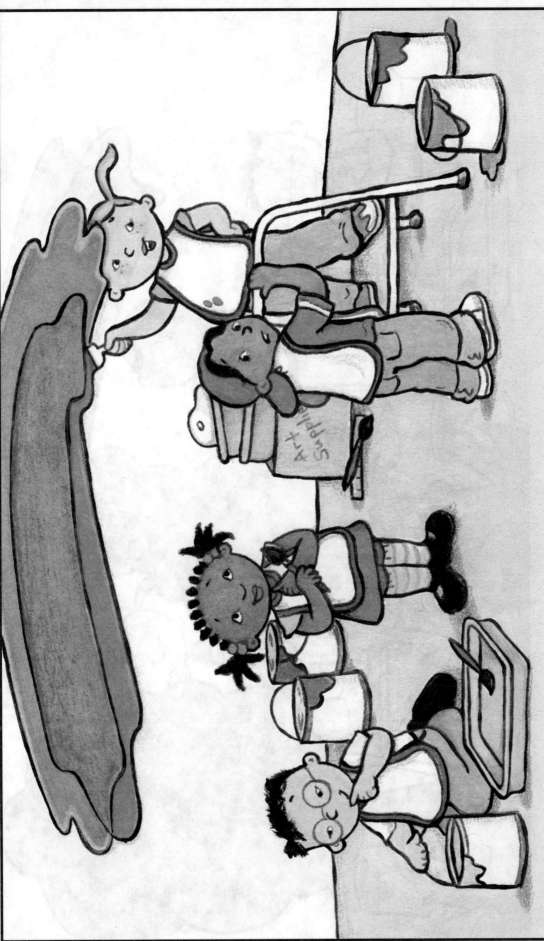

Across the hall to the paints
Zoe rushed
And opened a can of red.

With a look of disgust, she picked
up a brush.
"Oh, blue skies bore me," she said.

Jada sighed, "It's purple now,
Like sunsets I have seen."

With grins and giggles, she splashed
some wiggles
Of tall trees and grass with green.

Zoe stood in the hallway light   Then mixed red and white 'til it
And dropped her head to think,   looked just right
                                             And stabbed on flowers of pink.

Yuuto grinned and then began,   He poured a whole can in a metal pan
"I'm just the one for this job."   And daubed on a huge yellow blob.

"Your bright sun's too low,"
Zoe frowned.
"I really don't mean to scold."

So, close to the ground, she made it
less round,
And her bright orange strokes turned it gold.

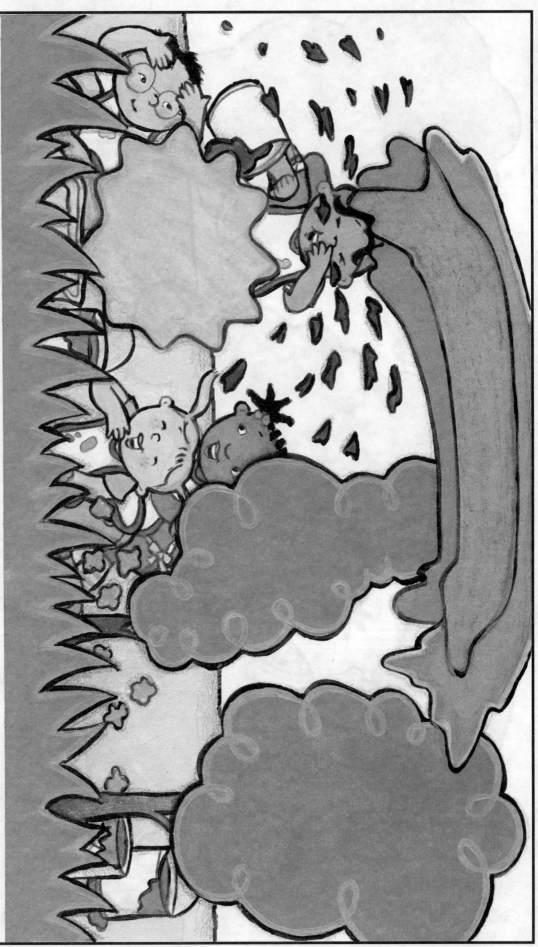

Eli started to paint a cow,
Perhaps an entire herd.
He was loaded with brown, but he sneezed anyhow,
And instead of cows, he had birds.

KE-804011 © Key Education

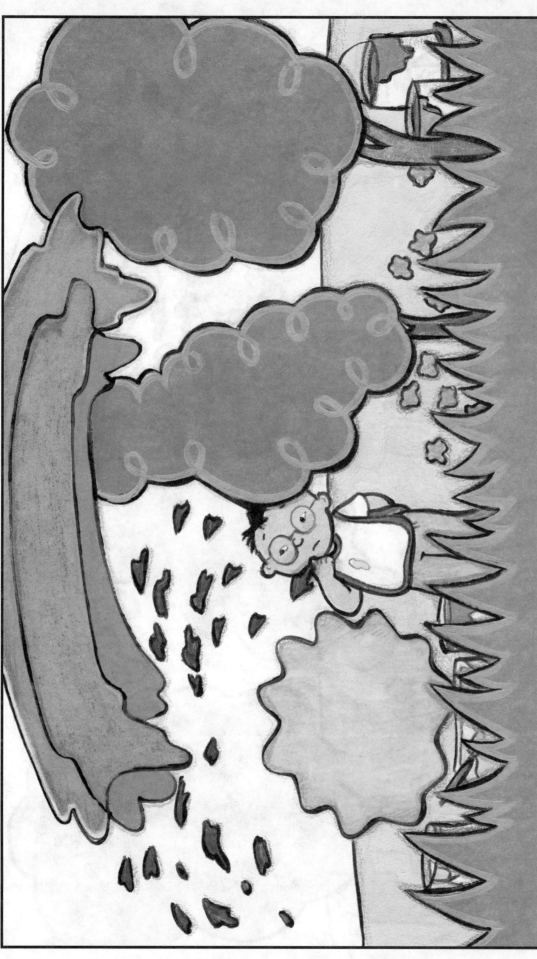

Yuuto said, "I really don't feel   It's not a big deal, but it doesn't look real,
This mural looks as it should.   And it's way too plain to be good."

They gathered close to the scene they'd done
And peered at its many parts.
Although they'd had fun, some thin paint had run.
All pride in their work left their hearts.

They silently turned away from their chore,
Toward their room and their books.

Across the floor and through the door,
Then turned again for one last look.

The Brainy Bunch Kids—Learning the Basics

The painting looked different from
that far away,
So blended from west to east.

In its own way, it was a kind
of Monet.
They smiled at their own masterpiece.

Name _____ **Date** _____

My Color Wheel

Directions: Use only red, blue, and yellow to color the wheel. Color the inside sections using the colors written on the outside ring. Some sections will need two layers of color.

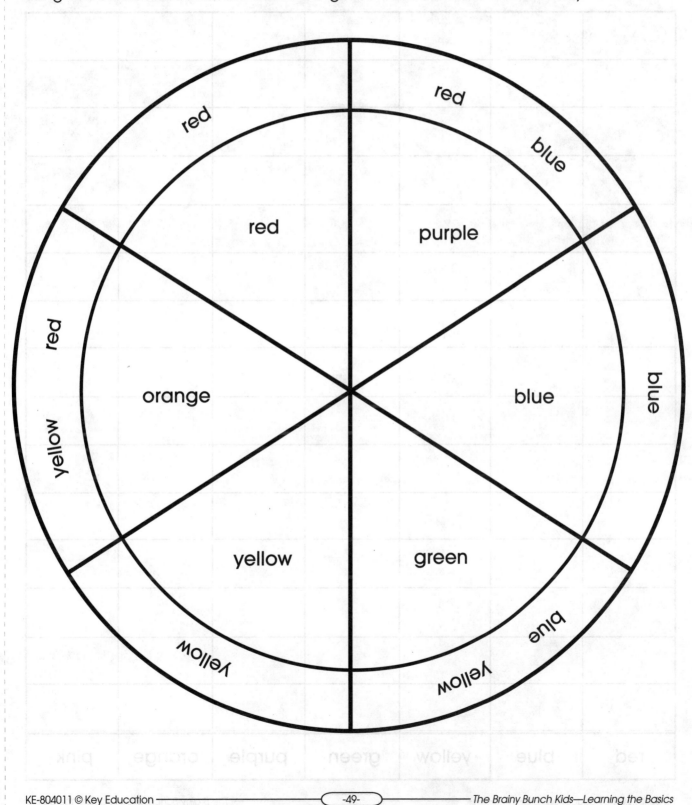

Name _____   **Date** _____

Favorite Colors Graph

Directions: Color each of the bottom boxes the correct color. Ask friends to write their names in the blank boxes above their favorite colors.

red	blue	yellow	green	purple	orange	pink

Name _____   **Date** _____

(See directions on page 35.)

Colorful Picnic

Directions: Listen carefully and follow directions to color the picture.

Name _____   Date _____

My Colorful Hike

Directions: Find something on your hike that is each color. Draw it in the correct box.

red	blue	green
yellow	orange	purple
pink	brown	black
white	favorite color	any color

Name _____   **Date** _____

Colorful Snacks

Directions: Cut out the snack pictures below on the dashed lines. Match each snack to its color. Glue it in the box. Then, color the snacks the correct colors.

red	yellow	green	pink
orange	purple	brown	white

Name _____   **Date** _____

I Can Print Color Words

Directions: Trace each color word with the same color of crayon. Then, use your pencil to print the words again.

red red _____

blue blue _____

yellow yellow _____

green green _____

purple purple _____

orange orange _____

brown brown _____

pink pink _____

white white _____

black black _____

Name _____   Date _____

Who Did What?

Directions: Listen carefully. Then, use the correct color to circle the correct Brainy Bunch kid or kids.

| Eli | Zoe | Jada | Yuuto |

1. Who painted the sky blue?

2. Who painted red streaks in the sky?

3. Who said the sky looked purple?

4. Who painted green grass?

5. Who mixed colors to make pink?

6. Who painted a yellow sun?

7. Who painted pink flowers?

8. Who painted with orange paint?

9. Who wanted to paint a brown cow?

10. Who said, "It's too plain to be good"?

11. At first, who was disappointed with the mural?

12. In the end, who was proud of the mural?

Name _____   Date _____

By the Seashore

Directions: Color code the numbers. Then, paint the picture by numbers.

- ☐ 1 = blue
- ☐ 2 = red
- ☐ 3 = yellow
- ☐ 4 = brown
- ☐ 5 = purple
- ☐ 6 = green
- ☐ 7 = orange
- ☐ 8 = pink

Chapter 3—Numbers
(Teacher's Guide)

Learning Center: Setting the Stage for the Pullout Story "The First School-Day Picnic"
Need: shelves or several small tables

Directions: To introduce and reinforce numbers, create a classroom mini-mart for counting from 0 to 12. As a backdrop for the learning center mini-mart, have students create a "picnic" bulletin board. (See below.) The center should contain a variety of empty food containers and toy (plastic) foods to count and sort, including the following:

- ❑ one large, plastic bowl
- ❑ two chip bags filled with crumpled paper and stapled shut
- ❑ three empty dip cartons with the lids taped on
- ❑ four plastic drumsticks
- ❑ five plastic eggs
- ❑ six-cupcake baking tin and play dough for making soufflés
- ❑ seven plastic hot dogs
- ❑ eight empty pudding boxes and a whisk or an eggbeater
- ❑ nine ice cream cones filled with colorful cotton balls of "ice cream"
- ❑ ten small paper plates painted or colored to look like pancakes
- ❑ eleven large paper plates painted or colored to look like pizzas

Bulletin Board: The Picnic
Need: bulletin board, roll of yellow paper, colorful construction paper—including black, 4" to 6" (10 cm to 15 cm) letter and number patterns, scissors, crayons, paints, stapler or tape

Getting Ready: Cover a bulletin board or wall with yellow paper. Trace letter and number patterns on black paper and cut them out to make the title and the numbers 1 through 12. Center the title at the top and evenly space the numbers across the board. Cut out 12 folded paper dolls from colorful paper to represent the last verse and attach them to the board.

Directions: Divide the class into 11 groups of various sizes. Assign each group a particular food or object listed in the Setting the Stage section above. Have each group draw, color, and cut out the appropriate number of objects. Attach the pictures to the board. The completed board may be used as a script while students rehearse An Action Story (page 58).

Snack: Foods to Count On
Caution: Before completing any food activity, ask families' permission and inquire about students' food allergies and religious or other food preferences.

Directions: Reinforce counting skills with one or more of these picnic, snack, or party ideas.

- ❑ Cooperate to make one bowlful of pineapple punch by combining pineapple juice, soda water, and chunks or rings of sliced pineapple. Count the floating ice cubes and pineapple chunks, the cups, etc.
- ❑ Make three kinds of dip to eat with two bags of chips. Children may count the chips as they eat.
- ❑ Make instant pudding and have students count to 12 as you whip the pudding with a whisk or turn the handle of an eggbeater. Then, ask, "Is it ready?" Repeat counting to 12 until the pudding has thickened.
- ❑ Use seven cooked hot dogs to count to seven. Cut the hot dogs into halves and count them again. Repeat until you have enough for everyone to sample.

Companion Book: *A Frog in the Bog*

"One tick in the belly of a small, green frog on a half-sunk log in the middle of the bog."

Need: *A Frog in the Bog* by Karma Wilson (Margaret K. McElderry Books)

Directions: Before reading the Brainy Bunch story, "The First School-Day Picnic," share the companion book. Then, reread the story and, with help from students, write on the board a numbered list from one to five of the frog's "picnic" (1 tick, 2 fleas, 3 flies, 4 slugs, 5 snails). Finally, invite students to illustrate the story—the frog, his lunch, and the alligator!

Other Good Books to Share:

❑ *City by Numbers* by Stephen T. Johnson (Viking)
❑ *Mooove Over! A Book About Counting by Twos* by Karen Magnuson Beil (Holiday House)
❑ *Mouse Went Out to Get a Snack* by Lyn Rossiter McFarland (Farrar, Straus and Giroux)
❑ *Two Bears Beneath the Stairs: A Lift-the-Flap Counting Story* by Elizabeth Spurr (Little Simon)

Presenting the Pullout Story: "The First School-Day Picnic"

Need: "The First School-Day Picnic" story (pages 63–74)

Directions: Present the Brainy Bunch story as a song, sung to the tune of "The Twelve Days of Christmas." Teach students the words and music. Then, sing the story/song together.

Drama: An Action Story

Need: "The First School-Day Picnic" story (pages 63–74), items as listed below

Directions: For a fun way to present the pullout story as a musical play, perform it as an action story. After each new action has been performed, the previous students repeat their actions counting backward to the first action.

1. Give 11 students (or 11 pairs or small groups of students) an action to perform or a sound to make.

    page 63—First child holds a plastic punch bowl high over her head.
    page 64—Second child shakes chip bags; then, first child holds up the punch bowl.
    page 65—Third child pretends to dip chips in carton; then, second shakes chip bags; etc.
    page 66—Fourth child flaps arms like a chicken; etc.
    page 67—Fifth child juggles plastic eggs; etc.
    page 68—Sixth child holds up cupcake pan and makes fizzling sounds; etc.
    page 69—Seventh child makes sizzling sounds; etc.
    page 70—Eighth child stirs the air with a whisk or turns the handle of an eggbeater; etc.
    page 71—Ninth child pantomimes licking a dripping ice cream cone; etc.
    page 72—Tenth child flips a small paper plate with a spatula; etc.
    page 73—Eleventh child spins a large paper plate like pizza dough; etc.
    page 74—All performers and teacher smile; etc.

2. Reread the story as students contribute their actions or sounds and rehearse as needed.
3. Present the story to a another class, to parents, or at a senior center.

Story Recall: Fingers Up

Directions: Begin by discussing the number *zero*. Show students how to sign the number *zero* by curving all four fingers into an O with fingertips touching the thumb. Then, tell students to listen carefully and answer the following questions about the story with a show of fingers.

1. How many doughnuts were dunking? *(0)*
2. How many kinds of dip were at the picnic? *(3)*
3. How many hot dogs were sizzling? *(7)*
4. How many bags of chips were there? *(2)*
5. How many deviled eggs were at the picnic? *(5)*
6. How many pancakes were flipping? *(10)*
7. How many ice creams were dripping? *(9)*
8. How many chicken legs were at the picnic? *(4)*
9. How many puddings were whipping? *(8)*
10. How many bowls of punch were at the picnic? *(1)*

Imagination: Picnic Math

Directions: Invite students to lie back and relax. Instruct them to close their eyes and listen carefully to try to see with their imaginations the colorful picnic you will describe. To give students time to use their visual memories and imaginations, pause 10–12 seconds after each description.

1. There is one red-and-white checked tablecloth on green grass. (pause)
2. In the center of the cloth are two watermelons. Each melon is cut into six slices. (pause)
3. There are four big sandwiches. See the brown peanut butter and purple grape jam? (pause)
4. There are three pink cakes, too. (pause)
5. Six cans of orange soda are in a cooler filled with ice. (pause)
6. Seven hot dogs with yellow mustard and green relish are on a red plate. (pause)
7. There is a pizza cut into 11 pieces. (pause)
8. Someone is flipping 10 blueberry pancakes. (pause)
9. In a yellow bowl, there are five deviled eggs. (pause)
10. On a green tray rest eight lemon pudding cups. (pause)

Follow-Up: After imagining the colorful foods, tell students you will give them time to think about their favorite picnic foods. (Allow three or four minutes.)

Critical Thinking: Name It

Directions: Gather students on the floor around you. Explain that you will give three clues about particular foods. When they think they know what you are describing, students should raise their hands. After giving all three of the clues for a food, ask someone with a raised hand to name it. Encourage a variety of creative answers.

	Clue 1	Clue 2	Clue 3
1.	served in a bowl	made with broth	chicken noodle is one kind (soup)
2.	cut into slices	often has cheese	pepperoni is a favorite (pizza)
3.	served in a cone	frozen	chocolate is one kind (ice cream)
4.	served at breakfast	covered with syrup	fried on a grill (pancakes)
5.	egg dish	yolk mixed with dressing	served in halves (deviled eggs)
6.	creamy dessert	made with milk	lemon is one kind (pudding)
7.	served on a bun	with mustard and ketchup	boiled or roasted (hot dogs)
8.	a meat dish	grilled or fried	part of a chicken called drumsticks (chicken legs)
9.	carried in a lunch box	ham and cheese is a favorite	two slices of bread (sandwich)
10.	a mixture of liquids	often fruit flavored	served from a large bowl (punch)
11.	put on ends of sticks	cooked over a fire	sweet and sticky (marshmallows)
12.	hot or cold liquid	sometimes includes a bag	served in a pot or with ice (tea)

Listening Skills: Guess the Number

Need: number line 0–12

How to Play: The first player thinks of a number 0–12. The other players take turns asking four yes or no questions. After the four questions have been answered, students hold up the number of fingers that indicate their guesses. (To indicate 11 and 12, have students open and close hands for 10 and then show one or two index fingers.)

Example for the number 7:
1. Is it more than 5? *(yes)*
2. Is it more than 10? *(no)*
3. Is it less than 8? *(yes)*
4. Is it more than 6? *(yes)*

Game: Number Concentration

Need: 3" x 5" (7.62 cm x 12.7 cm) index cards, black marker

Getting Ready: For each deck of cards, you will need 26 index cards. On each of 13 cards, print a number 0–12. Then, number the remaining 13 cards in the same way so that the deck contains a matching pair of each number.

How to Play:

1. Two to four players sit on the floor.
2. Shuffle the deck and place the cards facedown in four rows of six or seven cards in alternating rows.
3. Players take turns turning over two cards. If the cards match, and the player names the number, the player keeps the cards. If the cards match, but the player cannot name the number, the cards are turned facedown. If the cards do not match, the cards are turned facedown.
4. When all of the cards have been matched and collected, the player with the most cards wins the game.

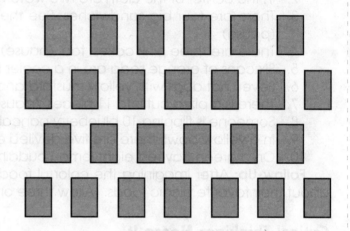

Game: BINGO

Need: BINGO reproducible (page 30); red, blue, and yellow crayons; sturdy black paper; paper cutter

Getting Ready:

1. Reproduce the BINGO card on page 30 for each student.
2. Cut the sturdy black paper into 1.5" x 1.5" (4 cm x 4 cm) paper chips to cover the BINGO squares. Give 25 chips to each student.
3. Have students randomly write the numbers 0–12 in red, blue, or yellow in the spaces on their cards but without repeating any number in the same color in a column under a letter. *Example: B*—red 5, red 6, blue 3, blue 10, and yellow 8. It would not be acceptable to color two red 5s under letter *B*.

How to Play: Randomly call a letter and then a color (red, blue, or yellow) and a number from 0–12. *Example: B*—yellow 10. Students will use paper chips to cover the corresponding squares on their cards. The first player to cover five in a row horizontally, vertically, or diagonally calls "BINGO!" and wins the game.

Snack: Class Picnic

Caution: Before completing any food activity, ask families' permission and inquire about students' food allergies and religious or other food preferences.

Need: large pizzas, paper plates, cups, plastic forks, blanket

Getting Ready: Let parents know that students are going to have a class picnic. First, have students share the Brainy Bunch story with parents. Then, ask parents to send five or six servings of one of the food items featured in the story for the picnic.

Directions: On the day of the picnic, take all of the food outside and place it on a blanket. Pass out paper plates and plastic forks. Invite students to serve themselves from the smorgasbord.

Directions for Reproducible Activity Pages

Story Recall: Color the Picnic—Page 75
Need: Color the Picnic reproducible (page 75), pencils or crayons
Directions: Reread the story, "The First School-Day Picnic." Pass out page 75. Demonstrate for students how to color or circle the correct number of foods in each row to complete the worksheet. Encourage them to use the pictures of the foods on the bulletin board or a number line if they need help. You may choose to pair students so that partners can help each other.

Language: Favorite Numbers—Page 76
Need: Favorite Numbers reproducible (page 76), pencils, crayons
Directions: On the board, draw a graph like the worksheet on page 76. Have students take turns naming their favorite numbers. Use the initials of students' first and last names to record the information on the graph. When the graph is complete, discuss the following questions.
1. Were any numbers not chosen as favorites?
2. Which numbers had the same number of votes?
3. Which number was the most popular?

After the discussion, pass out page 76. Explain that students should have at least 10 classmates write their initials in the boxes, each student writing in the column of his favorite number. Remind them to work from the bottom to the top of the graph. Then, to complete their graphs, have students color each square that has initials written in it.
Follow-Up: Meet as a large group to compare and discuss the graphs.
1. Are students' graph results similar to the graph created on the board?
2. Are students' graphs similar to each other?
3. Are any of the graphs identical?

Fine Motor: Picnic Paths—Page 77
Need: Picnic Paths reproducible (page 77), pencils, crayons
Directions: Pass out page 77. Explain that students should start at the top of the page and use a crayon to follow path A, counting the foods along the way. Then, they should record the number of foods in the circle at the end of the path. Have students choose a different crayon to follow each path as they complete the worksheet.
Follow-Up: Students may share their completed worksheets in small groups.

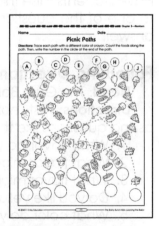

Following Directions: Colorful Numbers—Page 78
Need: Colorful Numbers reproducible (page 78); crayons in primary and secondary colors
Directions: Pass out page 78. Explain that you will give directions for coloring the numbers with different colors. Allow plenty of time for students to complete each step.
1. Color number *eight* with a red crayon.
2. Use a blue crayon to color number *three*.
3. Use a yellow crayon to color number *nine*.
4. Color number *five* with a green crayon.
5. Color number *seven* with a purple crayon.
6. Use a red crayon to color number *twelve*.
7. Color, with a yellow crayon, number *ten*.
8. Color number *zero* with a green crayon.
9. Color number *two* with purple.
10. Use an orange crayon to color *eleven*.
11. Color, with a red crayon, number *one*.
12. Color numbers *six* and *four* with blue.

Follow-Up: Pair students and have them correct their papers by comparing and discussing the numbers and colors.

Directions for Reproducible Activity Pages, CONTINUED

Outdoor Adventure: My Counting Hike—Page 79
Need: My Counting Hike reproducible (page 79), pencils, crayons
Directions: Pass out page 79. Then, have students take their worksheets and supplies outside. Explain that they should look for and then draw something they see that represents each number. Back in the classroom, have students verbalize their illustrations.
Examples:
I saw three trees.
I counted four rocks.
I found a trail with five ants.

Fine Motor: I Can Print Number Words and Numbers—Page 80
Need: I Can Print Number Words and Numbers reproducible (page 80), pencils
Directions: Pass out page 80. Read aloud the directions. Make sure students understand that first, they will trace each number word. Then, they will trace each numeral four times.

Story Recall: Which Was It?—Page 81
Need: Which Was It? reproducible (page 81), pencils
Directions: Reread the story "The First School-Day Picnic." Pass out page 81 and ask the questions as students follow along. Have students answer each question by circling the correct picnic food.

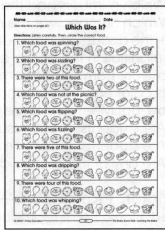

Follow-Up: After students have completed the worksheets, meet in large group. Again, read the story. Have students raise their hands when they hear the answer to one of the questions. Then, discuss each question and answer.

Following Directions: The Gum Ball Jar—Page 82
Need: The Gum Ball Jar reproducible (page 82), crayons in primary and secondary colors
Directions: First, hold a discussion about gum balls. Encourage a variety of responses by asking questions like the following:
1. What flavor do you think a blue gum ball might be?
2. What flavor might a purple gum ball be?
3. What flavor might a red gum ball be?
4. Do you like yellow gum balls? What flavor might a yellow gum ball be?
5. What color do you think a sour-apple flavored gum ball might be?
6. What color gum ball might also be the name of the flavor of the gum ball? *(orange)*

Pass out page 82. Make sure students have crayons in the primary and secondary colors. As you give directions, allow plenty of time for students to complete their coloring.
1. Color three gum balls red.
2. Use your orange crayon to color four gum balls.
3. Color five gum balls green.
4. Use your blue crayon to color seven gum balls.
5. Color eight gum balls purple.
6. Use your yellow crayon to color three gum balls.

Follow-Up: Pass out gum balls or colorful candies such as jelly beans. Have students count and name the colors before they enjoy the treats.

The First
School-Day Picnic

For the first school-day picnic,
The Brainy Bunch made lunch
With one bowlful of
pineapple punch.

Chapter 3—Numbers

The Brainy Bunch Kids—Learning the Basics

For the first school-day picnic,
The Brainy Bunch made lunch:
Two bags of chips,
With one bowlful of
pineapple punch.

For the first school-day picnic,
The Brainy Bunch made lunch:
Three kinds of dip,
Two bags of chips,
With one bowlful of
pineapple punch.

KE-804011 © Key Education

For the first school-day picnic,
The Brainy Bunch made lunch:
Four chicken legs,
Three kinds of dip,
Two bags of chips,
With one bowlful of
pineapple punch.

For the first school-day picnic,
The Brainy Bunch made lunch:
Five deviled eggs,
Four chicken legs,

Three kinds of dip,
Two bags of chips,
With one bowlful of
pineapple punch.

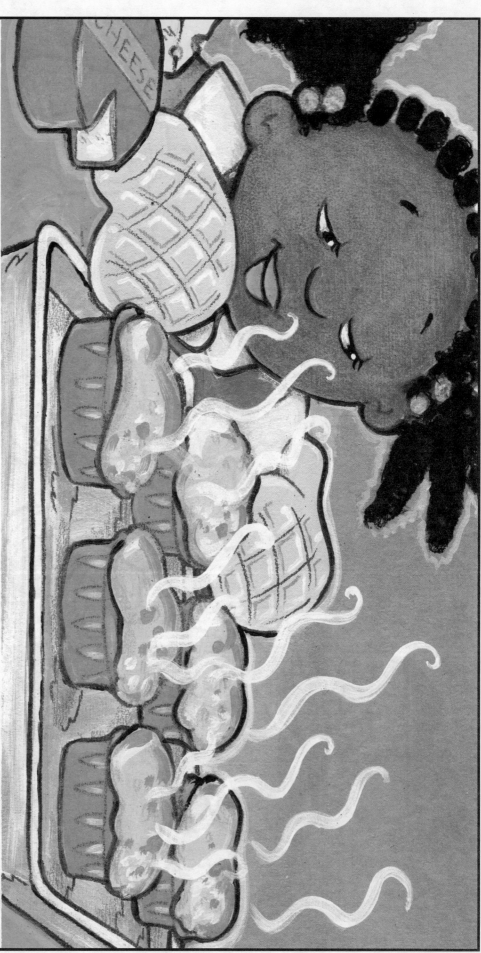

For the first school-day picnic,
The Brainy Bunch made lunch:
Six soufflés fizzling,
Five deviled eggs,

Four chicken legs,
Three kinds of dip,
Two bags of chips,
With one bowlful of pineapple punch.

For the first school-day picnic,
The Brainy Bunch made lunch:
Seven hot dogs sizzling,
Six soufflés fizzling,
Five deviled eggs,

Four chicken legs,
Three kinds of dip,
Two bags of chips,
With one bowlful of pineapple punch.

For the first school-day picnic,
The Brainy Bunch made lunch:
Eight puddings whipping,
Seven hot dogs sizzling,
Six soufflés fizzling,
Five deviled eggs,
Four chicken legs,
Three kinds of dip,
Two bags of chips,
With one bowlful of pineapple punch.

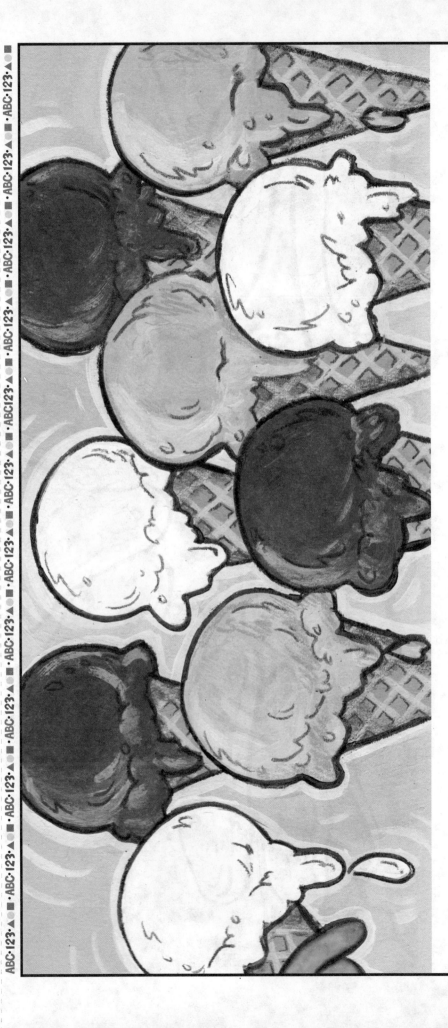

For the first school-day picnic,
The Brainy Bunch made lunch:
Nine ice creams dripping,
Eight puddings whipping,
Seven hot dogs sizzling,
    Six soufflés fizzling,

Five deviled eggs,
Four chicken legs,
Three kinds of dip,
Two bags of chips,
With one bowlful of
    pineapple punch.

For the first school-day picnic,
The Brainy Bunch made lunch:
    Ten pancakes flipping,
    Nine ice creams dripping,
    Eight puddings whipping,
    Seven hot dogs sizzling,

Six soufflés fizzling,
Five deviled eggs,
    Four chicken legs,
    Three kinds of dip,
    Two bags of chips,

        With one bowlful of pineapple punch.

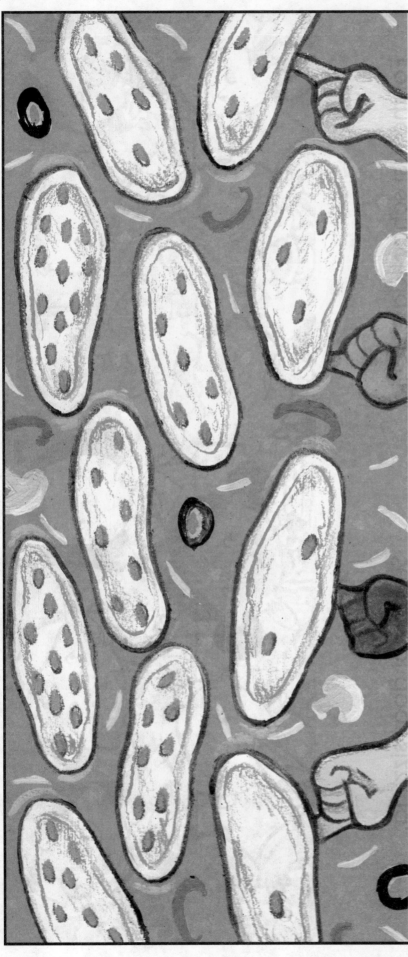

For the first school-day picnic,
The Brainy Bunch made lunch:
Eleven pizzas spinning,
Ten pancakes flipping,
Nine ice creams dripping,
Eight puddings whipping,
Seven hot dogs sizzling,
Six soufflés fizzling,
Five deviled eggs,
Four chicken legs,
Three kinds of dip,
Two bags of chips,
With one bowlful of pineapple punch.

The Brainy Bunch Kids—Learning the Basics

For the first school-day picnic,
The Brainy Bunch made lunch:
Twelve good friends grinning,
  Eleven pizzas spinning,
    Ten pancakes flipping,
  Nine ice creams dripping,
Eight puddings whipping,

Seven hot dogs sizzling,
  Six soufflés fizzling,
    Five deviled eggs,
      Four chicken legs,
        Three kinds of dip,
      Two bags of chips,

        With one bowlful of pineapple punch.

Name _____   **Date** _____

Color the Picnic

Directions: Read each number. Then, color or circle that number of foods.

2	(12 bags of chips)
4	(12 chicken legs)
8	(12 ice cream cups)
10	(12 cookies)
0	(12 donuts)
3	(12 dip cups)
11	(12 pizza slices)
5	(12 deviled eggs)
7	(12 hot dogs)
9	(12 ice cream cones)
6	(12 muffins)
1	(12 drink cups)

parseΚ

Name _____ **Date** _____

Favorite Numbers

Directions: Find your favorite number. Write your initials in the box above it. Then, ask at least 10 friends to write their initials in the boxes above their favorite numbers. To make a graph, color each box that has initials.

0	1	2	3	4	5	6	7	8	9	10	11	12

Name _____   **Date** _____

Picnic Paths

Directions: Trace each path with a different color of crayon. Count the foods along the path. Then, write the number in the circle at the end of the path.

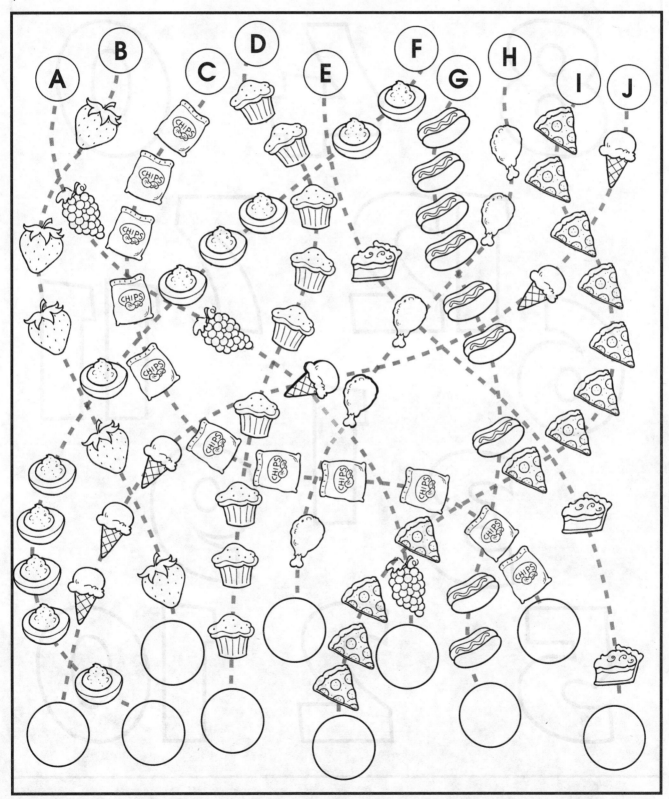

Name _____   **Date** _____

(See directions on page 61.)

Colorful Numbers

Directions: Listen carefully and follow directions.

Name _____   Date _____

My Counting Hike

Directions: Find and count something in nature for each number. Then, draw it in the correct box.

1	2	3
4	5	6
7	8	9
10	11	12

Name _____   **Date** _____

I Can Print Number Words and Numbers

Directions: Use a pencil to trace each number word. Then, trace each number four times.

one one	two two
1 1 1 1	2 2 2 2
three three	four four
3 3 3 3	4 4 4 4
five five	six six
5 5 5 5	6 6 6 6
seven seven	eight eight
7 7 7 7	8 8 8 8
nine nine	ten ten
9 9 9 9	10 10 10 10
eleven	twelve
11 11 11 11	12 12 12 12

Name _____ **Date** _____

(See directions on page 62.)
Which Was It?

Directions: Listen carefully. Then, circle the correct food.

1. Which food was spinning?

2. Which food was sizzling?

3. There were two of this food.

4. Which food was not at the picnic?

5. Which food was flipping?

6. Which food was fizzling?

7. There were five of this food.

8. Which food was dripping?

9. There were four of this food.

10. Which food was whipping?

Name _____ **Date** _____

(See directions on page 62.)

The Gum Ball Jar

Directions: Listen carefully and follow directions to color the gum balls.

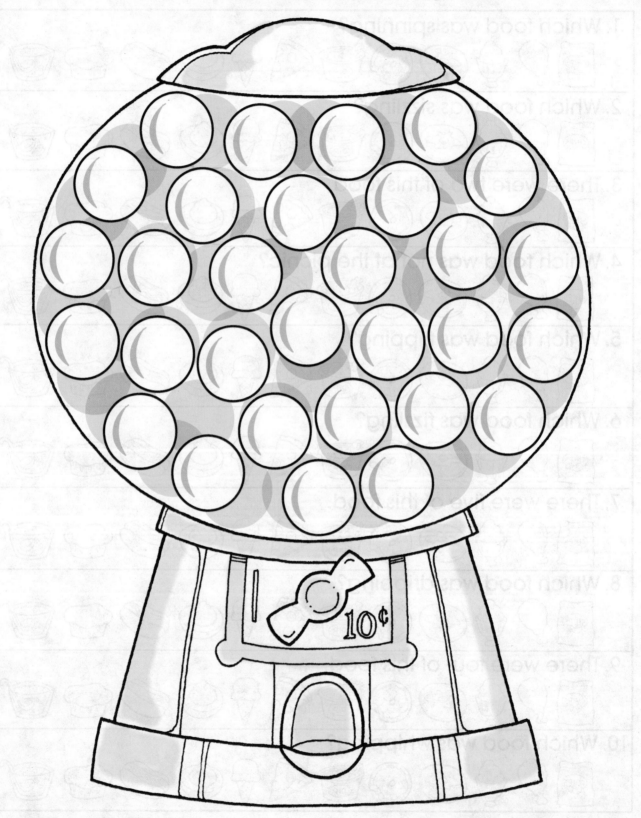

Chapter 4—Shapes
(Teacher's Guide)

Learning Center: Setting the Stage for the Pullout Story "Show-and-Tell Shapes"

Need: comfortable spot for playing on the floor with shape attribute cards and blocks

Directions: Set up a learning center where students can explore shapes. As a backdrop for the learning center, have students create a "Where the Wild Shapes Grow" bulletin board. (See directions below.) You may wish to include:

- ❏ companion book *Where the Wild Things Are*, story and pictures by Maurice Sendak (Harper & Row)
- ❏ several sets of shape attribute cards (directions on page 84 and patterns on page 107)
- ❏ wood building blocks (cubes, rectangular blocks, spheres, and prisms)

Companion Book: *Where the Wild Things Are*

"'And now,' cried Max, 'let the wild rumpus start!'"

Need: *Where the Wild Things Are*, story and pictures by Maurice Sendak (Harper & Row)

Directions: Before reading the Brainy Bunch story "Show-and-Tell Shapes," read aloud the companion book. This endearing classic is full of basic shapes. As you read and share the pictures, have students find and identify the various shapes.

Examples:

- ❏ Look at the ears of Max's wolf suit. How many sides do they have? *(three)*
- ❏ See the moon out of Max's window. What shape is it? *(round)*
- ❏ What shape is the rug in Max's bedroom? Door? Window? Bed? Pillow? *(rectangular)*

Other Good Books to Share:

- ❏ *Circle Dogs* by Kevin Henkes (Greenwillow Books)
- ❏ *Ship Shapes* by Stella Blackstone (Barefoot Books)
- ❏ *So Many Circles, So Many Squares* by Tana Hoban (Greenwillow Books)
- ❏ *Squares around Town* by Nathan Olson (Capstone Press)

Bulletin Board: Where the Wild Shapes Grow

Need: bulletin board; roll of blue paper; 12" x 18" (30.48 cm x 45.72 cm) colorful construction paper including black; 4" to 6" (10 cm to 15 cm) letter patterns; pencils; decorating supplies including paints, crayons, large precut shapes, etc.; scissors; stapler or tape

Getting Ready: Cover a bulletin board or wall with blue paper. Trace letter patterns on black paper and cut them out to make the title. Center the title at the top of the board. Create a forest by drawing or painting narrow, brown tree trunks reaching nearly to the top of the board. Position clumps of green, either cut from construction paper or painted, at the top of each trunk. Cut large, colorful shapes (circles, squares, triangles, and rectangles) from construction paper. Place the shapes on a nearby table with the decorating supplies.

Directions: To reinforce shapes in a big way, have students create this bulletin board. After sharing the companion book, *Where the Wild Things Are*, encourage students to use the colorful, basic shapes to make wild shape monsters. Encourage creativity; monsters might be hiding, dancing, sleeping, and so on. Attach the completed monsters to the board.

Presenting the Pullout Story: "Show-and-Tell Shapes"

Need: "Show-and-Tell Shapes" story (pages 89–100), colored chalk, colorful construction paper, scissors, United States flag

Directions: For an exciting and visual way to present "Show-and-Tell Shapes," follow these page-by-page directions. You may want to draw the shape outlines and other cut lines before beginning the presentation.

page 89—Draw a red triangle, circle, and square on the board.

page 90—Cut out a gray circle.

page 91—Cut out a gold or yellow circle.

page 92—Cut out a pink circle.

page 93—Cut out a blue puddlelike shape.

page 94—Cut out a large brown square. Then, cut the square into nine equal pieces.

page 95—Cut out a square and fold it in half. Then, beginning on the fold, cut another square out of the middle of the square. Unfold it to show the shape of a frame.

page 96—Trim a brown rectangular shape into a square.

page 97—Cut out a white square and hold it up like a rhombus. Then, turn it so that it is recognized as a square.

page 98—Cut out a red triangle.

page 99—Unfurl a United States flag. Ask a student to assist you.

page 100—Fold the flag lengthwise two times. Repeat triangular folds starting at the striped end and moving toward the blue field until the flag is completely folded.

Outdoor Adventure: Keep In "Shape" Hike

Directions: Take a hike around the school. Look for objects that are round, square, triangular, and rectangular. Have students take turns naming the shapes they see.

Follow-Up: Back in the classroom, have students draw four of the objects they saw—each student should depict something round, square, triangular, and rectangular.

Following Directions: Attribute Patterns

Need: Attribute Patterns reproducible (page 107); blue, red, and yellow sturdy paper; scissors; large envelopes

Getting Ready: For each student, reproduce page 107 on each color of paper—red, blue, and yellow. Have older students, aids, or parents help you cut out the sets of attribute patterns. Place each completed set of attribute patterns in a large envelope with a child's name on it. Each set must contain:

- ☐ three big circles (red, blue, and yellow)
- ☐ three small circles (red, blue, and yellow)
- ☐ three big squares (red, blue, and yellow)
- ☐ three small squares (red, blue, and yellow)
- ☐ three big triangles (red, blue, and yellow)
- ☐ three small triangles (red, blue, and yellow)
- ☐ three big rectangles (red, blue, and yellow)
- ☐ three small rectangles (red, blue, and yellow)

Directions: Have students place their patterns on desktops. Have each student hold up the correct size and color of each shape as you name it. *Example:* "Show me your big blue circle. Now, hold up your small yellow triangle." Store the attribute sets to be used in other games.

Discussion: Show-and-Tell Shapes

Directions: Set aside days for students to show and tell about objects in the following basic shapes. *Examples:*

Monday—circle   **Wednesday**—triangle   **Friday**—favorite shape day

Tuesday—square   **Thursday**—rectangle

Imagination: Think of That!

Directions: Invite students to lie back and relax. Instruct them to close their eyes and listen carefully to try to see with their imaginations the specific number of colored shapes you will describe. To give students time to use their visual memories and imaginations, pause 8–10 seconds after each description.

1. two black circles (pause)
2. three red squares (pause)
3. four white squares (pause)
4. two green rectangles (pause)
5. three pink triangles (pause)
6. zero yellow circles (pause)
7. one orange triangle (pause)
8. two blue triangles (pause)
9. three brown rectangles (pause)
10. two white triangles (pause)
11. three orange squares (pause)
12. one pink circle (pause)
13. two black rhombuses (pause)
14. five brown circles (pause)
15. a red triangle inside a blue circle (pause)
16. a pink square inside a yellow triangle (pause)
17. an orange circle inside a pink rectangle (pause)
18. three blue squares with red circle centers (pause)

Critical Thinking: Thumbs-Up

Directions: Gather students on the floor around you. Explain that you will name objects and describe the objects' shapes. If they think the object could be that shape, students should give a thumbs-up. Thumbs-down means the object is never that shape, for example, a square banana. Answers will vary. Encourage differing opinions by allowing time for discussion.

1. a square apple
2. a round table
3. a triangular road sign
4. a rectangular book
5. a round cake
6. a square pie
7. a triangular dollar bill
8. a square coin
9. a rectangular pillow
10. a triangular watermelon
11. a round bed
12. a round book
13. a square television
14. a square tree
15. a round starfish
16. a rhombus-shaped baseball
17. a round flag
18. a rectangular snowball

Follow-Up: Pair students and have them take turns challenging each other by naming objects and possible shapes.

Music: Sing the Shapes

Directions: Sing this song about shapes to the tune of "The Wheels on the Bus."

The wheels on the bus are nice and round,
Nice and round, nice and round.
The wheels on the bus are nice and round,
Spinnin' around the town.

The windows on the bus are square, not round,
Square not round, square not round.
The windows on the bus are square, not round,
Rattlin' around the town.

The doors on the bus are rectangular,
Rectangular, rectangular.
The doors on the bus are rectangular,
Bumpin' around the town.

The horn on the bus is triangular,
Triangular, triangular.
The horn on the bus is triangular,
Tootin' around the town.

Listening Skills: Yes or No?

Need: prepared sets of attribute patterns (See page 84 for directions.)

Directions: Reinforce the identification of attributes with a guessing game. Display the attribute patterns for visual reference as students play.

How to Play: The first player secretly chooses an attribute piece, for example, the big red circle. Students take turns asking yes or no questions. *Examples:* Is it big? *(yes)* Is it blue? *(no)* Is it round? *(yes)* The player who correctly guesses all three attributes (size, color, and shape) is next to secretly choose an attribute piece.

Critical Thinking: It's the Same

Need: prepared sets of attribute patterns (See page 84 for directions.)

How to Play: Gather students on the floor around you and pass out the sets of attribute patterns. Tell students to listen carefully to your directions. Then, they should follow each direction by holding up the correct attribute pattern. Explain that sometimes there will be more than one correct answer.

1. Hold up a big yellow circle. Say, "Show me one that is the same size." *(any big shape)*
2. Hold up a small red triangle. Say, "Show me one that is the same color." *(any red shape)*
3. Hold up a big blue square. Say, "Show me one that is the same shape." *(any square)*
4. Hold up a big red triangle. Say, "Show me one that is the same size and color, but not the same shape." *(big red circle, square, or rectangle)*
5. Hold up a small blue triangle. Say, "Show me one that is the same shape and color, but not the same size." *(big blue triangle)*
6. Hold up a small yellow square. Say, "Show me one that is the same shape and size, but not the same color." *(small square, either red or blue)*

Craft: All Together Now!

Need: Attribute Patterns reproducible (page 107), white paper, black construction paper, scissors, glue sticks

Getting Ready: Reproduce page 107 on white paper for each student.

Directions: Have students cut out the eight shapes. Then, each student should arrange the shapes on the black construction paper, overlapping shapes as desired. When students are pleased with their designs, they may glue the shapes to the black paper. Meet in large group to share and discuss the varied designs that were created.

Game: Attribute Rummy

Need: Attribute Patterns reproducible (page 107), colorful paper in three colors, card stock, paper cutter, glue stick

Getting Ready: Reproduce page 107 three times, each on a different color of paper for each deck of cards. Cut out the patterns. Cut the card stock into 4" x 4" (10 cm x 10 cm) squares. Make a deck of cards for each pair of players by gluing each of 24 colorful attribute patterns to a square of card stock.

How to Play: Divide students into pairs. Shuffle and deal each player eight cards. Players take turns drawing and discarding in an attempt to get two sets of cards. A set is four cards with patterns in the same color or size or shape.

Examples of rummy sets:
- four circles of any color or size
- any four shapes of one color
- any four small shapes

The first player with two sets calls "Rummy!" and wins the game.

Game: Shape and Color BINGO

Need: Shape BINGO reproducible (page 108); red, blue, yellow, green, purple, orange, pink, and brown crayons; sturdy black paper; paper cutter

Getting Ready:
1. Reproduce the BINGO card on page 108 for each student.
2. Cut the sturdy black paper into 1.5" x 1.5" (4 cm x 4 cm) paper chips to cover the BINGO squares. Give 25 chips to each student.
3. Have students randomly color the shapes on their cards using only the eight colors listed above.

How to Play: Randomly call a letter and then a color and shape. *Example: B—yellow square.* Students who colored the square under *B* yellow will use a paper chip to cover it. Continue calling letter-color-shape combinations. The first player to cover five squares in a row horizontally, vertically, or diagonally calls "BINGO!" and wins the game.

Directions for Reproducible Activity Pages

Field Trip Ideas: Sign Scavenger Hunt—Page 101

Need: Sign Scavenger Hunt reproducible (page 101), pencils, crayons

Directions: Look at the page 101 with students. Discuss the basic shape of each sign. Explain that they will take their papers home to help them go on a hunt for signs. As they are riding in a car, on a school bus, etc., or walking in their neighborhoods, they should look for each of the pictured signs and circle the ones they see.

Follow-Up: Back in class, meet as a large group for discussion.

1. Who found the most signs?
2. How many sides does a stop sign have?
3. How many signs were shaped like triangles?
4. Which signs were found most often?

Visual Discrimination: Shape Up!—Page 102

Need: Shape Up! reproducible (page 102), pencils, crayons,

Directions: Draw a circle, square, and triangle on the board. Begin by discussing the shapes of foods. Name a food and have students tell if its shape is basically round, square, or triangular.

Examples:

- whole pizza; slice of pizza
- meatballs
- whole orange; orange section
- whole cake; slice of cake
- cheese slice; cheese wedge

- whole pie; slice of pie
- meatloaf; slice of meatloaf
- whole apple; apple wedge
- saltine cracker; oyster cracker
- egg

After the discussion, pass out page 102. Help students color code the shapes by coloring each shape as indicated. Have students work independently to finish the worksheet. Culminate the activity by serving a treat cut into squares or triangles.

Following Directions: Color Carefully—Page 103

Need: Color Carefully reproducible (page 103), pencils, crayons

Directions: Explain that students should listen carefully and follow your directions to color each row of shapes. Repeat the directions as needed but say each row as a unit.

1. In the first row, color two squares green, one square orange, and one square red.
2. In row two, color one circle red and three circles yellow.
3. In row three, color one triangle blue, one triangle purple, and two triangles green.
4. In row four, color two rectangles orange, one rectangle red, and one rectangle blue.
5. In row five, color one circle red, one circle blue, and two circles yellow.
6. In row six, color one square yellow, two squares green, and one square orange.

Visual Memory: Draw and Color—Page 104

Need: Draw and Color reproducible (page 104), pencils, crayons

Directions: Have students draw the appropriate shape in each box and then color the shape as indicated. Allow time for students to complete the worksheets independently.

Follow-Up: Pair students. Have them check their work by comparing worksheets.

Fine Motor: Trace and Draw Shapes—Page 105

Need: Trace and Draw Shapes reproducible (page 105), pencils, crayons

Directions: Read aloud the directions. Make sure students understand that first they should trace each shape word. Then, they will trace the named shape three times. Allow time for students to draw and color their favorite shapes on the backs of their papers.

Directions for Reproducible Activity Pages, CONTINUED

Story Recall: Who Shared What?—Page 106
Need: Who Shared What? reproducible (page 106), pencils or crayons
Directions: Reread the story "Show-and-Tell Shapes." Pass out page 106 and read aloud each question. Have students answer each question by circling the correct Brainy picture or pictures.
Follow-Up: After students have completed the worksheets, meet in large group. Once again, read the story. Have students raise their hands when they hear the answer to one of the questions. Then, discuss the question and its answer.

Critical Thinking: Attribute Patterns—Page 107
Need: Attribute Patterns reproducible (page 107); white sturdy paper; orange, purple, and green crayons; scissors; large envelopes
Getting Ready: For each student, reproduce page 107 three times. Have each student color the eight patterns on one sheet orange, one sheet purple, and one sheet green. Help students cut out their colored patterns. Give each student an envelope for storing the patterns.
Directions: Have students spread out on the floor. Explain that they will each make a train with their patterns, working from left to right. Give directions as follows:
1. Put the big purple circle on the floor.
2. Next to the big purple circle, put the small green triangle.
3. Now, put down the big orange square.
Continue to give directions for building a train until all of the students' attribute patterns have been used.
Optional Activities:
1. Name a specific attribute shape. The first student to hold up the correct shape wins a point. Then, challenge students by naming both a specific shape and a color.
2. Build trains with each connecting pattern having one common attribute (color or size or shape).

3. Build trains with each connecting pattern having two common attributes (size and color, size and shape, or shape and color).

Following Directions: Shape BINGO—Page 108
Need: Shape BINGO reproducible (page 108), pencils, crayons
Directions: Pass out page 108. Have students listen carefully and color the shapes as directed. Repeat directions as needed and allow plenty of time for students to finish coloring each shape.
1. Color all of the rhombuses green.
2. Color the squares under the *B* and the *N* red.
3. Color the circle under the *I* orange.
4. Color the triangles under the *B* and the *O* purple.
5. Color the circles under the *N* and the *O* red.
6. Color the rectangles under the *B* and the *O* orange.
7. Color the circles under the *B* and the *G* orange.
8. Color the rectangles under the *I*, the *N*, and the *G* blue.
9. Color the triangles under the *I*, the *N*, and the *G* yellow.
10. Color the squares under the *I*, the *G*, and the *O* yellow.

Show-and-Tell Shapes

For show-and-tell, the teacher said,
"Each day a shape we'll share."

Then, on the board, she drew in red—
Triangle, circle, square.

KE-804011 © Key Education

ABC·123·▲◆■ · ABC·123·▲◆■ · ABC·123·▲◆■ · ABC·123·▲◆■ · ABC·123·▲◆■ · ABC·123·▲◆■ · ABC·123·▲◆■ · ABC·123·▲◆■ · ABC·123·▲◆■ · ABC·123·▲◆■

On circle day, Yuuto stood
where everyone could see.

"I'll play you something really good,
My favorite DVD."

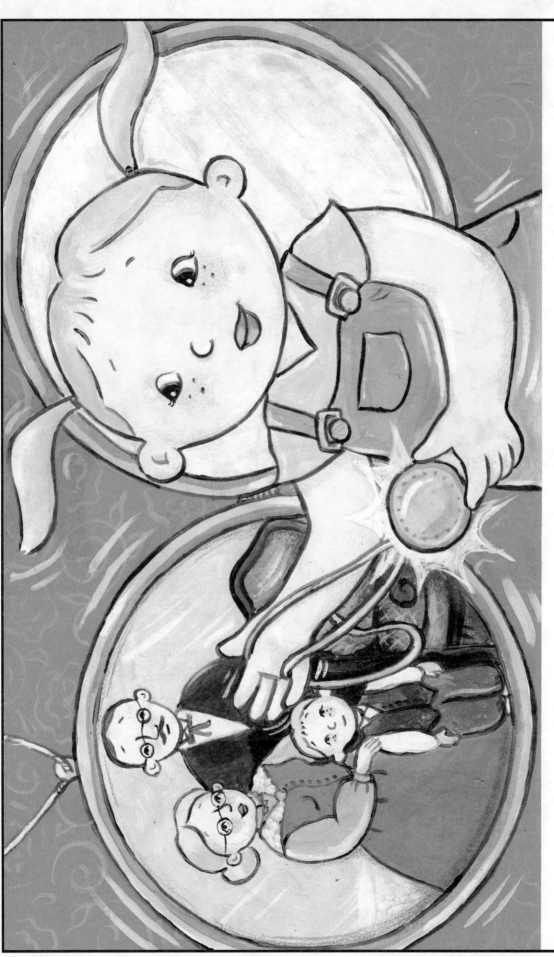

Zoe pulled a chain of gold   "Here's something round and very old,
That dangled from her pocket.   My great-great-grandma's locket."

Jada reached up to a shelf
And got a big peach pie.

"I made this pie all by myself.
It's baked, but some, I fry."

Eli showed a limp, wet bag.
He reached inside and felt it.

Then, he giggled at his little gag,
"I think my snowball melted."

The Brainy Bunch Kids—Learning the Basics

Jada baked a cake with nuts   She sliced it up with four long cuts
The day they showed their squares.   And gave all equal shares.

Zoe showed a photo frame.
"Here's my mom and I.

We live apart; no one's to blame.
Sometimes, it makes me cry."

Yuuto brought a piece of wood,
Longer than it was wide.

"I'll saw it 'til the length is good.
I measure my squares with pride."

Eli held a kitchen tile,
One corner raised in the air.

He leveled two sides and after awhile,
The rhombus became a square.

The Brainy Bunch Kids—Learning the Basics

Jada and Zoe on triangle day
Balanced a huge red and white sign.   "*Yield* means you give right-of-way
Or end up paying a fine."

KE-804011 © Key Education

Yuuto and Eli unfurled a flag   "But, that's a rectangle," the others said.
And held it aloft, full of pride.   "Triangles have only three sides."

The Brainy Bunch Kids—Learning the Basics

They grinned, and they started to fold, "A right triangle, so we've been told,
Is the way to fold our flag."
Zigzag, zigzag, zigzag.

Name _____   Date _____

Sign Scavenger Hunt

Directions: When you are in a car or on a school bus, look for these signs. When you see a sign, circle it.

Name _____   **Date** _____

Shape Up!

Directions: Color code the shapes to make a key. Then, color each food the same color as its shape.

Name _____   **Date** _____

(See directions on page 87.)

Color Carefully

Directions: Listen carefully and follow directions.

1.

2.

3.

4.

5.

6.

Name _____   **Date** _____

Draw and Color

Directions: Draw the shape. Then, color it the correct color.

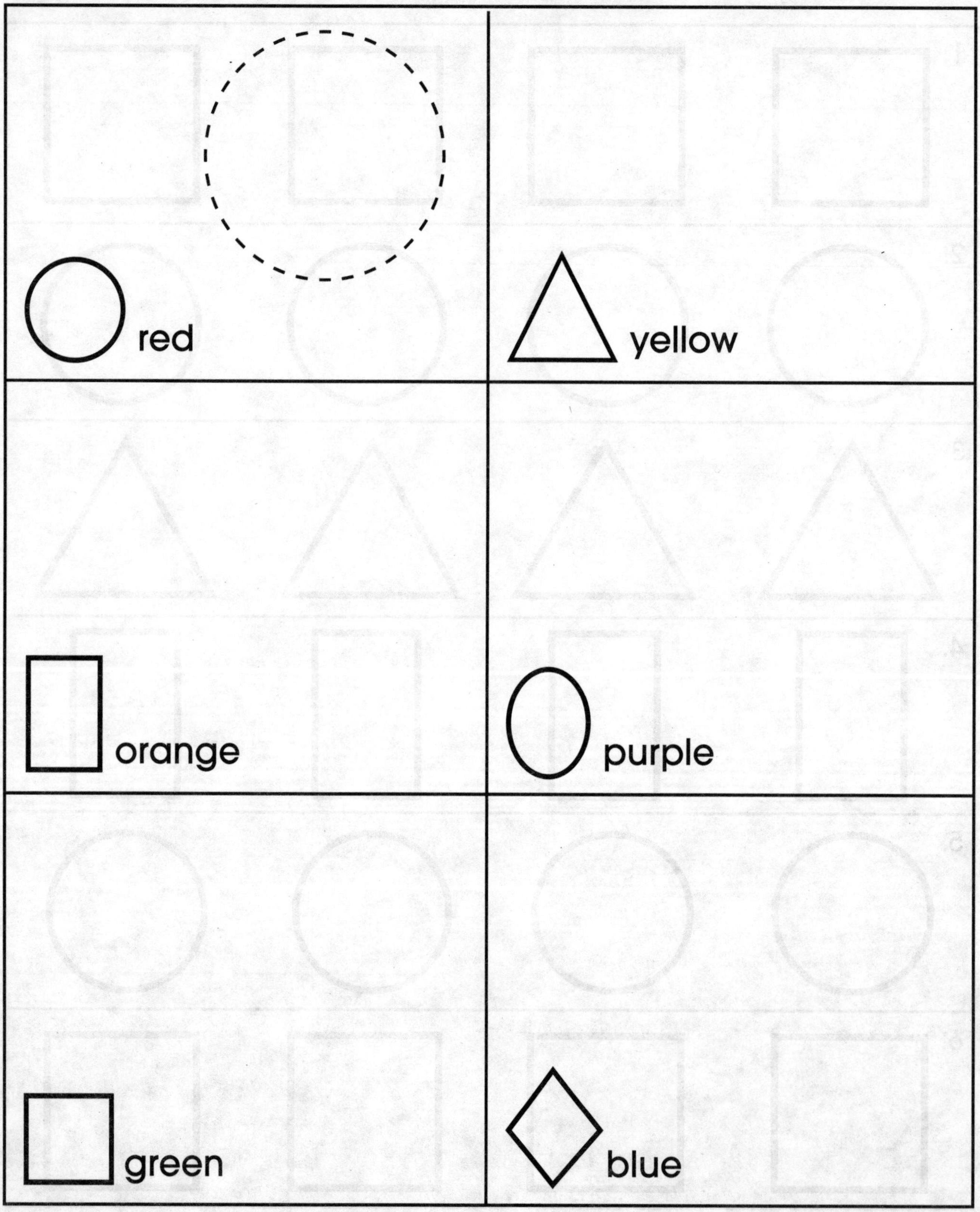

red

yellow

orange

purple

green

blue

Name _____ **Date** _____

Trace and Draw Shapes

Directions: Trace each shape word. Then, use your pencil to trace the shape. Next, draw and color your favorite shapes on the back of this paper.

circle

square

triangle

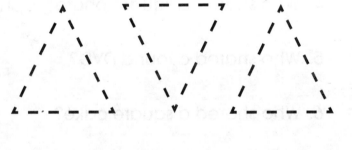

rectangle

rhombus

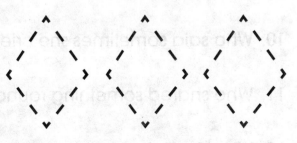

Name _____ **Date** _____

Who Shared What?

Directions: Listen carefully. Then, circle the correct Brainy Bunch kid or kids.

Eli   **Zoe**   **Jada**   **Yuuto**

1. Who shared a round locket?

2. Who shared a rectangular piece of wood?

3. Who shared folding a rectangle?

4. Who shared a square photograph?

5. Who shared a round DVD?

6. Who shared a square cake?

7. Who baked a peach pie?

8. Who made a square from a rhombus?

9. Who shared a triangular sign?

10. Who said sometimes she cried?

11. Who shared something round?

12. Who shared something square?

(See directions on pages 84–86 and 88.)

Attribute Patterns

(See directions on page 88.)   **Shape BINGO**   Name _____

B	I	N	G	O
☐	△	◇	△	◇
○	▭	△	○	▯
△	○	☐	◇	△
▯	◇	▭	▯	☐
◇	☐	○	☐	○

-108- *The Brainy Bunch Kids—Learning the Basics*

Chapter 5—Building Community and Character

(Teacher's Guide)

Learning Center: Setting the Stage for the Pullout Story "The Library Fund-Raiser"

Need: Sincere Compliments reproducible (page 133), Outstanding Character Award Certificate reproducible (page 134), pencils, scissors, small cardboard box with lid, comfortable gathering area

Getting Ready: Reproduce a stack of compliment slips and cut them apart. Cut a slit in the lid of the box. Place the slips, box, and pencils in the gathering area.

Directions: Values are the cornerstones of character. A learning center to celebrate values and good character and begin to build a sense of community might simply be a comfortable corner in which to gather to share sincere compliments, acknowledge acts of kindness, and present award certificates. Introduce the center by placing your own compliment and acknowledgement slips in the box. Let students know that their slips may be submitted either signed or unsigned. Since filling out the slips may prove too difficult for many youngsters, be available to help or enlist aids or older students to act as scribes. When completed, all of the slips go into the box. Daily, gather students around you. With great fanfare, pull out the compliment slips one at a time and read them aloud. Be aware of students who rarely receive recognition from classmates; you may wish to continue to add your own slips to the box. Culminate this community time by passing out a few award certificates.

Bulletin Board: Our Neighbors and Community Helpers

Need: bulletin board, roll of yellow paper, black construction paper, 4" to 6" (10 cm to 15 cm) letter patterns, scissors, stapler or tape

Getting Ready: Cover a bulletin board or wall with yellow paper. Trace letter patterns on black paper and cut them out to make the title. Center the title at the top of the board.

Directions: A bulletin board to reinforce community can be created with labeled photographs of favorite neighborhood friends and community workers such as a helpful dentist, an energetic clerk, a friendly janitor, etc. Encourage students to identify a variety of workers and the values they exemplify with questions and discussion.

Examples:
- ❏ Who knows a police officer? How would you describe him? Can you bring in a photo of him to share?
- ❏ Do you have a favorite helper here at school? Let's take a photo of her for our board.
- ❏ Does one of your parents work in a way that serves our community? Can you bring in a photo that shows the work?

Companion Book: *Miss Bindergarten Takes a Field Trip with Kindergarten*

"Today is field trip day . . . ."

Need: *Miss Bindergarten Takes a Field Trip with Kindergarten* by Joseph Slate (Dutton Children's Books)

Directions: Before reading the Brainy Bunch story, "The Library Fund-Raiser," share the companion book. This book reinforces not only community helpers but also simple shapes and the alphabet. With help from students, list on the board the places the kindergarten visited. *(bakery, fire station, post office, library, and park)*

Other Good Books to Share:
- ❏ *And to Think That We Thought That We'd Never Be Friends* by Mary Ann Hoberman (Crown Publishers)
- ❏ *Where Are You Going? To See My Friend!* by Eric Carle and Kazuo Iwamura (Scholastic)
- ❏ *Junie B., First Grader: Cheater Pants* by Barbara Park (Random House)
- ❏ *Edwurd Fudwupper Fibbed Big* by Berkeley Breathed (Little, Brown and Company)
- ❏ *A Fine, Fine School* by Sharon Creech (Joanna Cotler/HarperCollins)

Field Trip Ideas: Celebrate Community Helpers

Any of the following neighborhood excursions will celebrate community.

❑   police or fire station   ❑   doctor's or dentist's office
❑   senior center or nursing home   ❑   post office or library

Or, invite community helpers to visit your class. Allow plenty of time for students to talk with each guest.

Presenting the Pullout Story: "The Library Fund-Raiser"

Need: "The Library Fund-Raiser" story (pages 115–126), white construction paper, paper cutter, fine-tip black marker

Getting Ready: Cut 9" x 12" (22.86 cm x 30.48 cm) construction paper in half to make 4.5" x 12" (11.43 cm x 30.48 cm) cards. Make one card for each member of your class. In large letters, print one of the following adjectives on each card.

agreeable	courageous	fair	hardworking	kind	reliable
brave	curious	friendly	health minded	loving	respectful
caring	dependable	generous	helpful	patient	thoughtful
cheerful	eager	gentle	honest	pleasant	trustworthy
confident	energetic	glad	honorable	polite	unselfish
cooperative	enthusiastic	happy	hopeful	ready	willing

Directions: If students are to demonstrate good character, they must first know what characteristics are valued in relationships. The first step is to identify and be able to verbalize what makes a trait positive. Before reading the story aloud, have students take turns standing and holding up their word cards. Read each word together; then, ask questions to help students understand the word's meaning.

For the word *confident,* you might ask the following questions:

❑   What does *confident* mean?   ❑   Do you know a confident person?
❑   What makes you feel confident?   ❑   What is the opposite of feeling confident?

Collect and save the character word cards for Stand Up for Character (below) and Name That Characteristic (page 111). Read aloud the Brainy Bunch story "The Library Fund-Raiser." Then, have students name specific ways the Brainy Bunch demonstrated good character.

Discussion: Stand Up for Character

Need: character word cards (above)

Directions: Give each student a character word card. Have students stand as you review the word each student is holding. Reread the story one page at a time, stopping so that students holding the word cards with appropriate adjectives can stand up and tell who in the story demonstrated the positive character traits. Answers will vary; encourage creative discussion.

Examples:

page 115—The Brainies were confident, hopeful, enthusiastic, eager, willing, and ready.

page 116—Eli was cooperative, kind, fair, friendly, and thoughtful.

page 117—Zoe was cheerful and confident; the policeman was brave and courageous.

page 118—Jada's father was kind, helpful, loving, caring, willing, pleasant, and agreeable.

page 119—Jada was hardworking, energetic, and enthusiastic.

page 120—Yuuto's dentist was health minded.

page 121—Yuuto's dentist was fair, generous, and respectful.

page 122—Eli was polite and hopeful.

page 123—The fire chief was glad, agreeable, and pleasant.

page 124—Jada's doctor was thoughtful and generous.

page 125—Yuuto was honest, trustworthy, honorable, and patient.

page 126—The Brainies' teacher was happy, generous, and enthusiastic.

Language: Name That Characteristic

Need: character word cards (page 110)

Directions: Developing character involves the head (knowledge), the heart (desire/attitude), and the hands (behavior). Bridge the gaps between knowledge, desire, and behavior with this activity. Hold the character cards facedown in your lap and have children gather around you. Invite one student at a time to come forward. Show him the word on the top character word card. If he cannot read it, whisper the word in his ear. The student should then begin to give hints by making appropriate and descriptive statements about the word without using the word itself.

A student might give these hints for the word *helpful*:

☐ In the story, Jada's father was this.
☐ When I set the table I am being this.

Music: Won't You Be My Neighbor?

Getting Ready: Go online to http://pbskids.org/rogers/songlist/ to find the words to the following songs:

"Won't You Be My Neighbor?" "What Do You Do?"
"I'm Taking Care of You" "Let's Think of Something . . ."

Directions: Have students revisit the most famous neighborhood of all—Mr. Rogers' Neighborhood. Online, let students hear Fred Rogers sing all four of these wonderful songs. Then, teach students the words and melodies so that they can sing along!

Drama: Were They Good Neighbors?

Directions: Use fairy tales to discuss and playact character development. Begin by telling one of the fairy tales listed below. Then, divide the class into groups of four students. Explain that each group will create a short skit about the story. Allow plenty of time for students to practice their dramas. Have each group perform its skit for the class. Discuss both positive and negative traits demonstrated by the various characters in the skits.

☐ "The Little Red Hen" *(hardworking; lazy)*
☐ "The Three Billy Goats Gruff" *(cooperative, courageous; fearsome, cruel)*
☐ "The Boy Who Cried Wolf" *(helpful; dishonest)*
☐ "Cinderella" *(obedient, cheerful, hardworking, hopeful; greedy, unkind)*
☐ "Goldilocks and the Three Bears" *(disrespectful of others' property)*
☐ "The Three Little Pigs" *(caring for and sharing with siblings; frightening)*
☐ "Little Red Riding Hood" *(helpful; disobedient)*
☐ "Snow White" *(friendly, loving, helpful; jealous)*

Music: Sing About Character

Directions: Write on the board the positive-characteristic words (listed on page 110) that contain two syllables: *caring, cheerful, eager, friendly, gentle, happy, helpful, honest, hopeful, loving, patient, pleasant, polite, ready, thoughtful,* and *willing.* Then, review the chorus of the song "I've Been Workin' on the Railroad."

Someone's in the kitchen with Dinah. *Fee, fie, fiddle-e-i-o.*
Someone's in the kitchen, I know. *Fee, fie, fiddle-e-i-o-o-o-o.*
Someone's in the kitchen with Dinah *Fee, fie, fiddle-e-i-o.*
Strumming on the old banjo. *Strumming on the old banjo.*

Choose a student—one who exemplifies one of the characteristics written on the board—to stand. Next, tell students which characteristic you will be singing about.

Example: patient

Someone in our classroom is patient. *Fee, fie, fiddle-e-i-o.*
Someone in our classroom, we know. *Fee, fie, fiddle-e-i-o-o-o-o.*
Someone in our classroom is patient. *Fee, fie, fiddle-e-i-o.*
(Student's name) is patient—it shows. *(Student's name) is patient—it shows.*

-111-

Critical Thinking: Who or Where?

Directions: Gather students on the floor around you. Explain that you will give three clues about either a community worker or a community building. When students think they know who or what you are describing, they should raise their hands. After giving all three clues, ask someone with a raised hand to name the community worker or building. Often, there will be more than one correct answer. Encourage a variety of answers.

Clue 1	Clue 2	Clue 3
1. uses a red vehicle	sleeps at a station	puts out fires (firefighter)
2. works in an office	has an assistant	fixes teeth (dentist)
3. belongs to a troop	wears a uniform	sells cookies (Girl Scout)
4. place where people meet	often serves lunches	senior citizens are here (senior center)
5. place where people are kept	people call here for help	place where police officers are (police station)
6. place where sick people go	doctors and nurses work here	place where people get better (hospital, doctor's office)
7. place with food	waiters and cooks work here	people eat here (restaurant)
8. place with children	teachers work here	place where students learn (school)

Listening Skills: Guess What My Daddy Does

Directions: Gather students around you. Pick someone to begin the game. This first player silently thinks of a person she knows, such as her father, mother, or neighbor, and that person's profession. Then, the player says, "Guess what my _____ does." Other students take turns asking yes and no questions to determine the chosen person's profession. The first student to guess correctly thinks of the next person and profession.

Language: Small Deeds of Kindness May Lead to Great Friendships

Directions: Read the following short story aloud.

The Bee and the Robin

A bee was at the bank of a stream drinking when he was washed away by the water. The bee was at the point of drowning when a robin that had been singing on an overhanging branch plucked a leaf and dropped it into the stream for the bee. The bee scrambled onto the leaf and floated safely to the bank. For days after, the bee thought about the robin. He wondered how he could ever repay her for saving his life. Then one day, the bee got his chance. It was autumn and hunting season. Although hunters never shoot robins, some cruel boys do. It was nearly dusk when a boy came into the woods sporting a rifle. When the boy saw the robin, he lowered himself onto one knee and took careful aim. The bee knew the boy's intention, and he dropped onto the boy's arm and stung him. The boy yelled, "Ouch!" And, hearing the noise, the robin flew safely away.

Discuss the story with the following questions:
1. Are bees and robins usually friends?
2. Why did the bee want to be friends with the robin?
3. Why do you think the robin saved the bee's life?
4. Have you ever had someone whom you did not know very well do something kind for you, and then you became good friends?
5. Who is your best friend?
6. What kind things do you do for your best friend? What does your friend do in return?

Follow-Up: Share the Aesop's fable "The Lion and the Mouse."

Directions for Reproducible Activity Pages

Craft: Tools of the Trade—Page 127

Need: Tools of the Trade reproducible (page 127), scissors, glue sticks, pencils, crayons

Directions: Pass out page 127 and discuss each tool pictured at the bottom of the page. Have students cut out the tools on the dashed lines and glue each tool in the box with the matching community worker.

Bulletin Board: Family, Our Nearest Neighbors—Page 128

Need: My Family reproducible (page 128), bulletin board, roll of white paper, black construction paper, 4" to 6" (10 cm to 15 cm) letter patterns, pencils, crayons, markers, scissors, stapler

Getting Ready: Cover a bulletin board with white paper. Trace letter patterns on black paper and cut them out to make the title. Center the title at the top of the board.

On a whiteboard or chart paper, list the positive character traits found on page 110. Then, pass out page 128 to the class.

Directions: Have each student draw the people who live in her home. Help students write a positive characteristic under each person in their drawings. Cut out the drawings along the dashed lines and mount them on 9" x 12" (22.86 cm x 30.48 cm) black construction paper. Then, attach these "framed" family portraits to the bulletin board.

Story Recall: Who Did What?—Page 129

Need: Who Did What? reproducible (page 129), "The Library Fund-Raiser" story (pages 115–126), pencils, crayons

Directions: Reread the story "The Library Fund-Raiser." Pass out page 129 and read aloud each question as students follow along. Have students answer each question by circling the correct Brainy picture or pictures.

Follow-Up: After students have completed the worksheets, meet in large group. Once again, read the story. Have students raise their hands when they hear an answer to one of the questions. Then, discuss the question and its answer.

Fine Motor: Fund-Raiser Maze—Page 130

Need: Fund-Raiser Maze reproducible (page 130), pencils, crayons

Directions: Pass out page 130 and discuss where each Brainy Bunch kid went to sell candy. Have students trace each of the Brainies' paths.

Follow-Up: In large group, review students' work with the following discussion questions.

1. Who sold candy to the dentist? *(Yuuto)*
2. Who saw Girl Scouts? *(Eli)*
3. Whose father wanted to help? *(Jada's)*
4. Who went back to school for more candy? *(Jada)*
5. Who went to the senior center? *(Eli)*
6. Who went to the fire station? *(Zoe)*
7. Who went to a doctor's office? *(Jada)*
8. Who sold candy to a policeman? *(Zoe)*

Directions for Reproducible Activity Pages, CONTINUED

Critical Thinking: Wheel of Character—Page 131

Need: Wheel of Character reproducible (page 131), pencils, paper, scissors

Directions: Pass out page 131. Explain that the rim, or outside edge, of the wheel represents character. The spokes represent positive character traits; these give the wheel form, shape, and strength. The hub, which is the circle in the center that holds the spokes in place, represents the individual. Have students draw or paste photos of themselves inside the hub in the center of their wheels. Help each student list six of his most outstanding positive character traits on the spokes. Then, have students illustrate the ways they demonstrate each characteristic. When students have completed their character wheels, they may cut them out.

Follow-Up: Share the character wheels in large group setting. Ask each student to give an example of behavior that demonstrates one of the positive character traits shown on her wheel.

Connecting with Family: Portrait of Good Character—Page 132

Need: Portrait of Good Character reproducible (page 132), pencils, crayons

Directions: Invite students to think about a person whom they admire. Discuss what characteristics students think are admirable in these people. Then, send page 132 home with students. Each student should draw a picture of a person he admires. Ask parents to help list positive character traits of the person on the back of the student's drawing and send it back to school.

Follow-Up: When papers are returned to class, take time to share pictures and discuss each chosen person's positive character traits. Ask each student to give an example of how her person demonstrates one of the positive characteristics.

Language: Sincere Compliments—Page 133

Need: Sincere Compliments reproducible (page 133), pencils

Directions: Discuss compliments and how it feels to receive a sincere compliment. Then, pass out a compliment slip to each student. Help students write compliments to classmates. You may also choose to contribute compliments, being sensitive to any students who have not received a compliment from a classmate. Read aloud some of the compliments.

Optional Activities:

1. Help students write compliments to a parent or sibling and take them home to share.
2. Help students write compliments to school helpers—janitors, aids, student teachers, the principal, etc. Then, deliver the compliments.
3. Help students write compliments to community helpers—firefighters, police officers, librarians, etc. Then, mail the compliments.

Surprise Activity: Award Certificate—Page 134

Need: Outstanding Character Award Certificate reproducible (page 134), pencils

Directions: Each day for one week, discuss outstanding characters in the categories below. After introducing each category, list on the board students' choices for people in that category with positive character traits.

Examples:

Monday—in the family (siblings, mother, father, grandparents, uncles, aunts)

Tuesday—in the neighborhood

Wednesday—in the community (firefighters, police officers, mayors, dentists, doctors, librarians)

Thursday—at school (aids, helpers, student teachers, principals, secretaries, janitors)

Friday—in the world (presidents, humanitarians, religious leaders)

After each student has selected an award-winning character, have her fill out an award certificate for the chosen person. Then, help students deliver or mail the awards.

The Library Fund-Raiser

They thought it was dandy,
a plan to sell candy
Raising the money for books.

"We'll sell the most,"
The Brainies did boast,
And two cartons apiece they each took.

When Eli went out, he met some
Girl Scouts
Selling their cookies in pairs.

"It would be great
To cooperate.
You stay here; I'll sell over there."

A policeman nearby, Zoe did spy,
And flagged him down with a wave.

"Which kind will you take?
It will help you stay awake
Tonight, when you're keeping us safe."

117

Jada's nice father said, "Hey, it's no bother.
I'll take these two cartons to work.

We can make a big sign,
Make it look fine,
And sell candy to all of my clerks."

Jada went to get more, out through
   the door,
And walked back to school—
   seven blocks.

It's worth it, she thought.
We need a whole lot.
I'm going to sell one more box.

The Brainy Bunch Kids—Learning the Basics

Yuuto's young dentist looked up
with interest,
"Let ME give YOU candy instead.

If your teeth decay,
The more you must pay,
And the quicker that I'll get ahead."

"That's really not true, I respect
     what you do;
A library should be complete.

To be fair to you,
     I'll buy one or two
For my father, who must wear false teeth."

121

Eli entered the new senior center.
His grandpa was there playing pool.

"Is it okay
To sell here today?
Will your friends support our school?"

The fire chief's eyes lit up with surprise.
He said, his voice full of glee,

"What a good snack!
Please, Zoe, come back.
Altogether, I'll buy two or three."

KE-804011 © Key Education

The Brainy Bunch Kids—Learning the Basics

KE-804011 © Key Education

Jada's doctor, old Doctor Proctor,
Said, "Really, it does seem to me

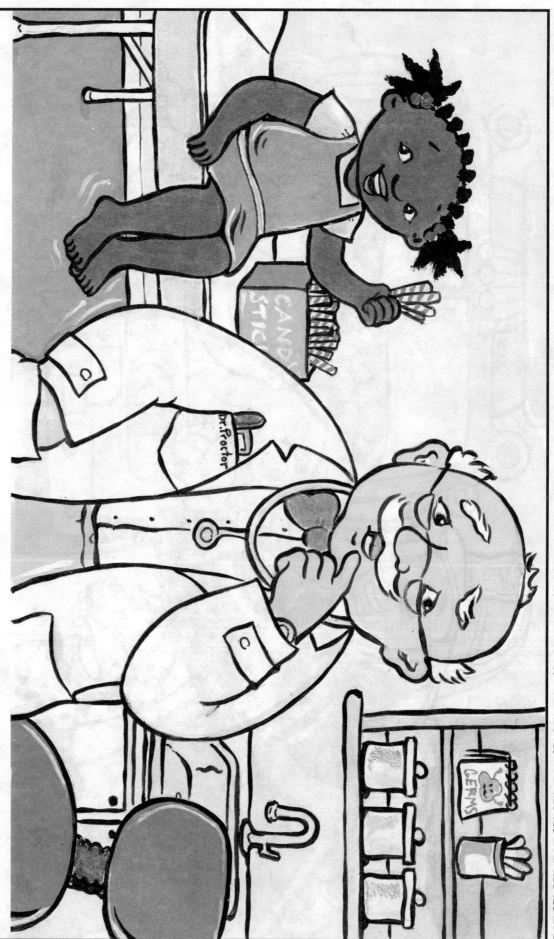

The thought of a library
With too few books is scary.
I'm thinking that I will buy three."

I wish I at least could have one little piece.

But if I don't do what's right, I'll feel lousy tonight;

Yuuto thought, no one would know. And no candy's worth feeling so low.

The teacher said, "Yes, this class
    did their best.
The fund-raiser now is done.

    I've brought you a treat
        To share after we eat—
Some candy. Great job, everyone!"

Name _____ **Date** _____

Tools of the Trade

Directions: Cut out the tools below on the dashed lines. Glue each tool in the correct box.

(See directions on page 113.)

my family

Name _____ **Date** _____

Who Did What?

Directions: Listen carefully. Then, circle the correct Brainy Bunch kid or kids.

Eli **Zoe** **Jada** **Yuuto**

1. Who felt hungry for candy?

2. Who thought they could sell lots of candy?

3. Who was energetic and went back for another box?

4. Who was polite and asked permission to sell?

5. Who cooperated with Girl Scouts?

6. Who sold three candies to a doctor?

7. Who had help from her father?

8. Who asked a policeman to buy candy?

9. Who sold candy to a fire chief?

10. To whom did the teacher give candy?

11. Who probably sold the most boxes of candy?

12. Who had some trouble selling candy?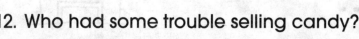

Name _____ **Date** _____

Fund-Raiser Maze

Directions: Trace the path each Brainy Bunch kid took in the story.

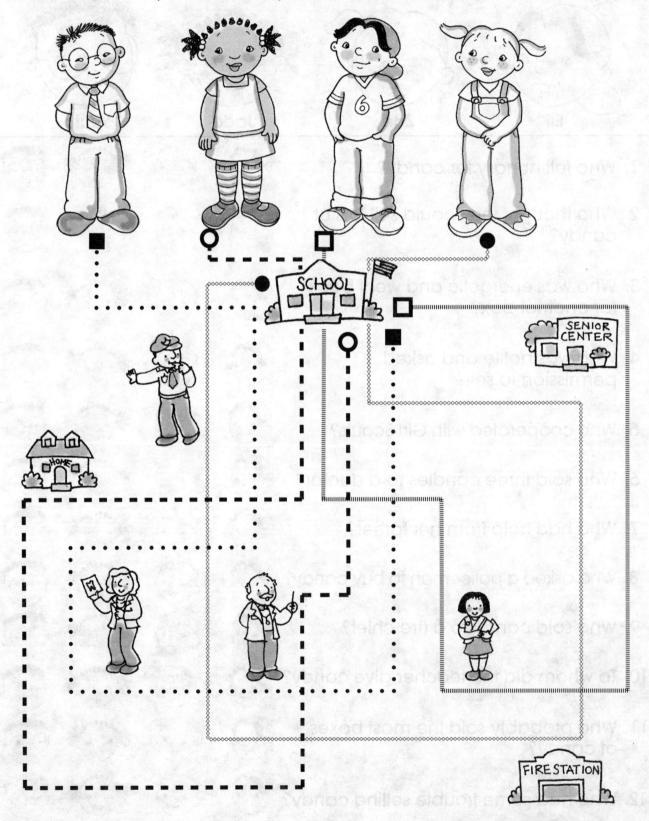

Name _____ **Date** _____

Wheel of Character

Directions: Draw or paste a photo of yourself in the center. Choose six of your positive character traits. Write one on each spoke of the wheel. Then, draw yourself showing each positive trait.

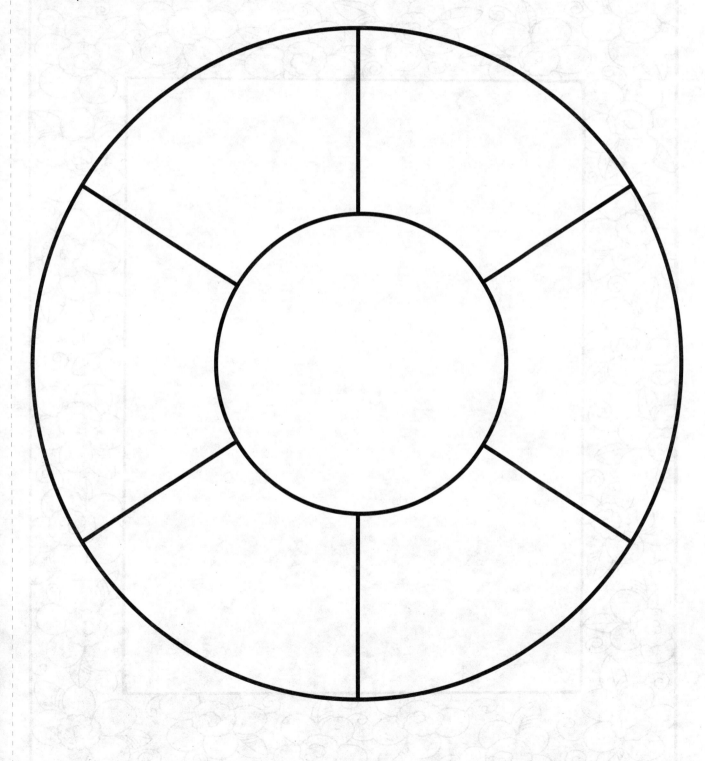

Name _____   **Date** _____

Portrait of Good Character

Directions: Draw the face of someone you know who shows great character. Ask an adult to help you list the person's good character traits on the back of this paper.

A sincere compliment

Presented to

_____

A friend acknowledges you for

_____

_____

From: _____

Date: _____

A sincere compliment

Presented to

_____

A friend acknowledges you for

_____

_____

From: _____

Date: _____

A sincere compliment

Presented to

_____

A friend acknowledges you for

_____

_____

From: _____

Date: _____

A sincere compliment

Presented to

_____

A friend acknowledges you for

_____

_____

From: _____

Date: _____

Award Certificate

presented to

in recognition of

Outstanding Character

Signature:

Date:

Chapter 6—Prepositions
(Teacher's Guide)

Learning Center: Setting the Stage for the Pullout Story "The Hat Mystery"
Need: comfortable spot for relaxing and playing on the floor with books, blocks, and position word cards

Directions: Set up a learning center to celebrate 14 basic positions: on, off, in, through, out, next to, between, under, over, around, far, near, up, down. The center should include:
- companion book—*Where's Waldo?* pictures and words by Martin Handford (Candlewick Press)
- other Waldo titles—*Find Waldo Now, The Great Waldo Search,* and *Where's Waldo? The Ultimate Fun Book!*
- *Where's Waldo* featuring harder to find Waldos (Candlewick Press) and a magnifying glass
- colorful building blocks
- position word cards (page 160)

Companion Book: *Where's Waldo?*
"My name is Waldo. I'm just setting off on a worldwide hike. You can come too."

Need: *Where's Waldo?* pictures and words by Martin Handford (Candlewick Press)

Directions: Before reading the Brainy Bunch story, "The Hat Mystery," share the companion book. *Where's Waldo?* will provide many opportunities to discuss positions. Each double-page illustration can easily become a whole activity session. If possible, secure enough copies of the book so that students may work together in small groups of three or four. Present each mystery on the pages and ask additional questions that will reinforce positions. The following are examples for the first full-page illustration:

1. What is the man **on** the roof feeding? *(birds)*
2. What is falling **off** the window washer's scaffold? *(bucket of water)*
3. What animal is **in** the window of the apartment **above** the shoe shop? *(cat)*
4. What color car is parked **in front of** the school? *(red)*
5. What shop is **next to** the wrecked car and truck? *(bookstore)*
6. What happened to the men coming **out of** the barbershop? *(they got short haircuts)*
7. What is found **between** the police station and the electronics store? *(fire station)*
8. What is **under** the manhole cover? *(man)*
9. What is the man holding a load of dishes about to trip **over**? *(dog's leash)*
10. What are the people **outside** the electronics store looking at **through** the window? *(TV)*
11. What vehicle is **around** the corner from the hotel? *(blue bus)*
12. Is the school **far from** or **near** the man playing the violin? *(far from)*

Other Good Books to Share:
- *All About Where* by Tana Hoban (Greenwillow Books)
- *Elephants Aloft* by Kathi Appelt (Harcourt Brace)
- *Over-Under* by Catherine Matthias (Children's Press)
- *Two Bears Beneath the Stairs: A Lift-the-Flap Counting Story* by Elizabeth Spurr (Little Simon)

Presenting the Pullout Story: "The Hat Mystery"
Need: "The Hat Mystery" story (pages 141–152), Position Word Cards reproducible (page 160), sturdy paper, paper cutter

Getting Ready: Reproduce enough copies of page 160 on sturdy paper so that each student will have a word card. Cut apart the words.

Directions: Read aloud the Brainy Bunch story "The Hat Mystery." Then, read aloud the position word cards and give one to each student. As you read the story again, students should quickly stand up and sit back down when they hear their words. Have students exchange cards. Read the story one more time while students listen for their new position words.

Discussion: Talk About a Mystery!

Directions: Taking time to show each picture, reread "The Hat Mystery." Follow with a discussion.

1. What do you think happened to the hat? List students' ideas on the board.
2. Have you ever lost something? What?
3. How do you feel when you lose something?
4. How do you feel when you find something that you thought you had lost?
5. Have you ever found something that didn't belong to you and returned it to its owner? How did that make you feel?

Bulletin Board: The Hike Mural

Need: bulletin board; roll of light green paper; black construction paper; 4" to 6" (10 cm to 15 cm) letter patterns; scissors; pencils; paint, crayons, markers, and/or colored chalk; stapler or tape

Getting Ready: Cover a wall or bulletin board with light green paper. Trace letter patterns on black paper and cut them out to make the title. Center the title at the top of the board.

Directions: To reinforce the meanings of position words, illustrate "The Hat Mystery" on a bulletin board. Reread the story. Assign the following specific objects or people to students: Zoe, Jada, Eli, Yuuto, the teacher, grass, worms, bugs, brook, brush, rocks, trees, fallen boughs, leaves, fence posts, bus, cows, and straw hat. Then, have students draw and color their people and objects.

Follow-Up: When the mural has been completed, point to each illustration as students verbalize the position words from the story.

Listening Skills: Where Are They?

Directions: Show each page of "The Hat Mystery" one at a time, stopping to ask the following questions:

1. Who raced **around** the trees? *(Yuuto)*
2. Who searched **near** the edge of the brook? *(Jada)*
3. Who looked **under** some brush? *(Zoe)*
4. Who looked **behind** a rock? *(Zoe)*
5. Who climbed **up** a tree? *(Eli)*
6. Who looked **through** leaves? *(all of the Brainies)*

Outdoor Adventure: Hide-and-Go-Seek Hat

Need: straw hat

Getting Ready: Go outside to play a game of "hide-and-go-seek hat."

How to Play:

1. Have students close their eyes as you hide the hat.
2. Tell children to look for the hat. When a child finds it, she should not touch it or announce its location. She should simply run back to a prearranged base and sit down.
3. When everyone has returned to the base, the first child to return describes where the hat was found. *Example:* The hat is behind the big rock beside the tree. Then, that child retrieves and hides the hat for the next round of play.

Field Trip Ideas: Bug Hunt

Need: pencils and paper

Directions: What will be a good excursion to celebrate positions? A hike to look for bugs and worms in the grass, of course! Go to a backyard, park, woods, pond, ranch, or farm to look for bugs and worms. Have students draw the animals they find, including the creatures' positions in relation to the surrounding rocks, trees, and so on.

Follow-Up: Back in class, meet as a group and have students show their drawings and describe where they found their bugs. *Examples:* My cricket was under a branch on the ground. This dragonfly was beside the pond.

Imagination: Imaginary Pictures

Directions: Invite students to lie back and relax. Instruct them to close their eyes and listen carefully to try to see with their imaginations the objects and their positions you will describe. To give students time to use their visual memories and imaginations, pause at least 10 seconds after each description.

1. a red apple **inside** a blue bag (pause)
2. a pink balloon bobbing **in** the air (pause)
3. an orange **outside of** a box (pause)
4. three stars shining **through** a window (pause)
5. a green circle **between** two red circles (pause)
6. a red sun **over** the blue ocean (pause)
7. a star **far from** a full moon (pause)
8. a rope wrapped **around** a tree trunk (pause)
9. a yellow pear **on top of** a blue plate (pause)
10. a yellow circle **inside** a red rectangle (pause)
11. a red triangle **next to** a blue circle (pause)
12. a yellow thread **through** the eye of a needle (pause)
13. a pink cloud **between** two red clouds (pause)
14. a red ribbon tied **around** a present (pause)
15. green grass **near** a lake (pause)
16. a red fish **under** the ocean (pause)

Critical Thinking: Thumbs-Up

Directions: Gather students on the floor around you. Explain that they should listen carefully to your statements. If they think the statement is true, they should give a thumbs-up. Thumbs-down means the statement is false. After each thumbs-down statement, ask students to change the position word or words to make the statement true.

1. You look **up** to see the sky.
2. You look **down** to see the sun.
3. Your ears are **between** your eyes.
4. Your knees are **under** your feet.
5. Your nose is **on** your face.
6. When dressing, you take **off** your clothes.
7. To leave your house, you go **out of** the door.
8. A yellow yolk is **inside** an egg.
9. A roof is **underneath** a house.
10. You live **next to** your neighbor.
11. You look **through** glass windows.
12. Your elbows are **between** your ears.
13. You can hide **under** your bed.
14. You sail **over** the ocean in a boat.
15. You go **around** corners.
16. China is **far from** the United States.
17. Your head is **near** your feet.
18. You climb **up** the hill to the top.
19. The moon is **near** the earth.
20. A tree's roots are **below** the ground.

Following Directions: Simon Says

Directions: Reinforce the meanings of position words by playing Simon Says. Have students sit down to play this version of the game with the following directions. Then, let students take turns giving directions to their classmates.

1. Simon says, "Take **off** one shoe."
2. Simon says, "Put your shoe back **on**."
3. Put your hands **between** your knees.
4. Simon says, "Touch **beneath** your chin."
5. Simon says, "Put your hands **behind** your back."
6. Put a finger **in** each ear.
7. Simon says, "Look **out of** the window."
8. Simon says, "Smile at the person **next to** you."
9. Simon says, "Look at someone **near** you."
10. Look at something **far from** you.
11. Simon says, "Look **up**."
12. Look **down**.
13. Simon says, "Thumbs **up**."
14. Simon says, "Thumbs **down**."
15. Wink at the person **in front of** you.
16. Simon says, "Lean to your **left**."
17. Simon says, "Lean to your **right**."
18. Simon says, "Put your hands **in** the air."
19. Look all **around** you.
20. Look **down** at the floor.
21. Simon says, "Touch **under** your foot."
22. Simon says, "Put your hands **in** your lap."

Music: Old MacDonald's Barn

Need: Position Word Cards reproducible (page 160), Short and Long Vowel Animal Picture Cards reproducible (page 263), scissors

Getting Ready: Reproduce the position word cards and animal picture cards on sturdy paper. Cut apart the cards and place the word cards and picture cards in separate stacks.

Directions:

1. Explain to students that they will sing new words to the tune of "Old MacDonald Had a Farm"; the new song's title is "Old MacDonald Had a Barn."
2. One at a time, hold up and read aloud each position word card.
3. Then, show each animal card and discuss the sound each type of animal makes:
   - mules—bray   goats—bleat   sheep—baa   hens—cluck   ducks—quack
   - mice—squeak   pigs—oink   cats—meow   snakes—hiss   dogs—bark
4. Draw the top card from each stack and display them as you sing the verse together. Repeat with a new position word and animal picture for each verse.

 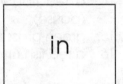    

Old MacDonald had a barn, E-I-E-I-O.
*And **in** his barn he had a **cat**, E-I-E-I-O*
With a "meow, meow" here
*   and a "meow, meow" there,*
Here a "meow," there a "meow,"
Everywhere a "meow, meow."
Old MacDonald had a barn, E-I-E-I-O.

Old MacDonald had a barn, E-I-E-I-O.
*And **near** his barn he had some **sheep**, E-I-E-I-O*
With a "baa, baa" here
*   and a "baa, baa" there,*
Here a "baa," there a "baa,"
Everywhere a "baa, baa."
Old MacDonald had a barn, E-I-E-I-O.

Visual Memory: Where Do You Find It?

Directions: Ask questions that require position word answers. Responses will vary, but each answer must contain an appropriate preposition.

1. Name a place you can find a fire. (***in*** *a fireplace*)
2. Where do you wear a hat? (***on*** *my head*)
3. Where can you find a bridge? (***over*** *water*)
4. Where is your nose located? (***between*** *my eyes*)
5. When threading a needle, where does the thread go? (***through*** *the hole*)
6. Where might you find a rubber ducky? (***in*** *a bathtub*)
7. Where is the roof of a house? (***on top of*** *the house*)
8. Your fingers are found where? (***at the end of*** *my hand*)
9. Where do you sit on a bus? (***in*** *the seat*)
10. Where is the beach? (***next to*** *the ocean*)
11. Where is the sun? (***far from*** *the earth*)
12. Where is your neighbor's house? (***next to*** *our house*)

Critical Thinking: Name It

Directions: Gather students on the floor around you. Explain that you will choose an object in the room and give three clues about where the object is. Students should listen carefully to the clues and then take turns guessing which object you chose. Repeat the series of clues or give additional position clues as needed.

Example: It is **above** a window, **below** the ceiling, and **on** the same wall as the clock.

Directions for Reproducible Activity Pages

Following Directions: Old MacDonald's Barn—Page 153

Need: Old MacDonald's Barn reproducible (page 153), scissors, glue sticks, pencils, crayons

Directions: Pass out page 153. Explain that students should listen carefully and color the picture according to your directions. Allow plenty of time for coloring.

1. Inside old MacDonald's barn is a big animal. Color it brown. *(mule)*
2. Near old MacDonald's barn is a woolly animal. Color it black. *(sheep)*
3. Under old MacDonald's barn is a hissing animal. Color it purple. *(snake)*
4. On old MacDonald's barn is Mrs. MacDonald's pet. Give her pet yellow stripes. *(cat)*
5. Around old MacDonald's barn are pesky animals. Color them blue. *(mice)*
6. Near old MacDonald's barn is a pond. Color the animal in the pond green. *(duck)*
7. Up in the hayloft is an animal that lays eggs. Color it red. *(hen)*
8. Lying down beside old MacDonald's barn is Mr. MacDonald's pet. Give his pet blue spots. *(dog)*
9. Outside old MacDonald's barn is an animal in the grass. Color it gray. *(goat)*
10. In a mud puddle in old MacDonald's yard is an animal. Color it pink with brown spots. *(pig)*

Story Recall: Who Said or Did It?—Page 154

Need: Who Said or Did It? reproducible (page 154), pencils

Directions: Reread aloud the story "The Hat Mystery." Pass out page 154 and ask the questions as students follow along. Have students answer each question by circling the correct Brainy picture or pictures.

Follow-Up: After students have completed the worksheets, meet in large group. Again, read the story. Have students raise their hands when they hear an answer to one of the questions. Then, discuss the question and its answer.

Following Directions: Drawing Positions—Page 155

Need: Drawing Positions reproducible (page 155), pencils

Directions: Pass out page 155. Explain that you will give directions for drawing in each box. Then, read aloud each direction as students follow along. Allow plenty of time for students to complete each drawing.

1. Draw a bug under the chair.
2. Draw a bird over the cloud.
3. Draw stars all around the moon.
4. Draw a baseball in the hand.
5. Draw another mouse down in the corner.
6. Draw a hat on the head.
7. Draw a cat far away from the cow.
8. Draw a flower near the duck.
9. Draw a dog between the two boys.
10. Draw a potato next to the carrot.

Connecting with Family: What Goes There?—Page 156

Need: What Goes There? reproducible (page 156)

Directions: Pass out page 156 and read the directions together. Explain that students will take home the page and ask parents to help them think of something that goes where each word directs. Then, students should draw their answers and return the papers to school.

Examples:

1. **through**—thread going through the eye of the needle
2. **on top of**—candles on top of the cake
3. **under**—water under the bridge
4. **over**—frog jumping over the rock
5. **inside**—anything inside the box
6. **next to**—jam next to the bread
7. **between**—a block labeled *B* between block *A* and block *C*
8. **around**—thread wrapped around the spool

Follow-Up: Back in class, allow time for students to share their papers and discuss the answers.

Directions for Reproducible Activity Pages, CONTINUED

Snack: Order Please—Page 157

Need: Order Please reproducible (page 157), pencils, presliced loaf of bread, waxed paper, rolling pins, plastic knives, jam in small cups

Directions: Pass out page 157. One at a time, look at each row of pictures. Explain that students should decide which happens first, second, and last in each row. Have students work independently to write 1, 2, or 3 in the boxes to indicate the order of events. Then, gather as a large group and discuss students' answers.

Follow-Up: Have students make jam rolls. Write the directions (below) on the board. Give each student a piece of waxed paper for a working surface, one slice of bread, a plastic knife, and a small amount of jam in a cup.

1. Cut crust from bread.
2. Roll bread flat.
3. Spread with jam.
4. Roll up like a jelly roll.
5. Cut into 3 slices.
6. Enjoy!

Caution: Before completing any food activity, ask families' permission and inquire about students' food allergies and religious or other food preferences.

Story Recall: Where Is the Teacher's Hat?—Page 158

Need: Where Is the Teacher's Hat? reproducible (page 158), glue sticks, scissors

Directions: Pass out page 158. Read aloud the directions and each position word to students. Have students finish the page independently.

Following Directions: Cut and Paste in Place—Page 159

Need: Cut and Paste in Place reproducible (page 159), scissors, glue sticks, crayons

Directions: Pass out page 159. Have students cut out the six animal pictures at the bottom of the page. Explain that you will tell them where to paste each picture. Read the directions below, allowing plenty of time for pasting and coloring.

1. Put the snail exactly in the middle of the page.
2. Put the skunk between the hippo and the duck.
3. Put the frog next to the fox.
4. Put the zebra under the duck.
5. Put the bird beneath the snail.
6. Put the hen over the snail.
7. Color the animal above the sheep orange.
8. Color the animals in the top row blue.
9. Color the snail and the animal directly beneath the snail yellow.
10. Color the rest of the animals red.

Game: Position Word Cards—Page 160

Need: Position Word Cards reproducible (page 160), scissors

Getting Ready: Cut apart one page of word cards to use as an example.

Directions: Teach students the hand movements below for each word card word. Then, one at a time, hold up word cards as students do the hand movements. If needed, say each word as you hold it up. Shorten the time between words as students respond more quickly with the correct movements. Pass out page 160 and have students cut the word cards apart on the dashed lines. Pair students and have them take turns showing the cards to their partners and making the hand movements.

around—use one hand to circle around the other hand

between—touch hands to cheeks

down—point down with the pointer finger

far—hold hands as far apart as possible

in—move one hand into the other hand

near—hold palms up without hands touching

next to—hold palms up with hands touching

off—move one hand off of the other hand

on—move one hand on top of the other hand

out—point out the door

over—hold one palm up; move the other hand over it

through—slide one hand through the separated fingers of the other hand

under—hold one palm up; move one hand under it

up—point up with the pointer finger

The Hat Mystery

On a warm day,
The teacher took the class

In search of worms
And bugs in the grass.

But right off the bat,
The teacher lost her straw hat.

Caught in the wind,
It was gone—like that!

Zoe said, "Come on,
It will be all right."

And off the kids went,
Right out of sight.

The Brainy Bunch Kids—Learning the Basics

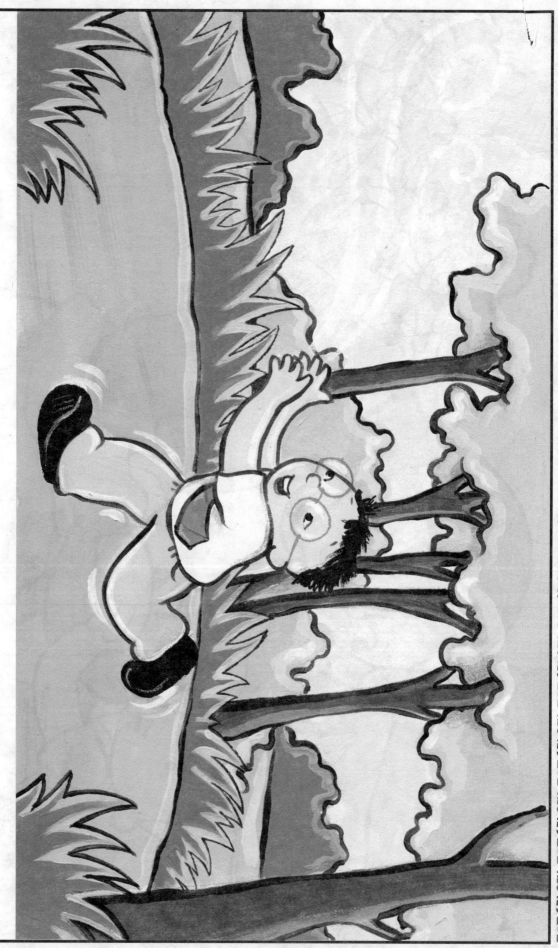

Around the tall trees,
Yuuto raced.

But of the teacher's straw hat—
He found not a trace.

KE-804011 © Key Education

Near the brook's edge,
Jada searched in vain.

She walked up and down,
Again and again.

Under some brush,
Behind a rock, too,

Zoe found nothing—
Not one clue.

From up in a tree,
Eli looked down.

But the lost hat
Was nowhere around.

They looked through leaves and
Between fallen boughs

Next to the fence posts
That kept in the cows.

Over and under,
Far and wide—

"It can't disappear!"
Jada cried.

149

After awhile,
The teacher said, "Whoa!

Our bus is here;
It's time to go."

KE-804011 © Key Education

Climbing the steps to their seats,
The kids looked sad as they sat.

But their teacher said,
"It's just a straw hat."

The bus pulled out
Nice and slow,

And Eli sighed,
"Guess we'll never know."

Name

Date

Old MacDonald's Barn

Directions: Listen and follow directions to color the picture.

(See directions on page 139.)

Name _____   **Date** _____

Who Said or Did It?

Directions: Listen carefully. Then, circle the correct Brainy Bunch kid or kids.

Eli   **Zoe**   **Jada**   **Yuuto**

1. Who looked behind a rock?

2. Who looked under brush?

3. Who looked next to fence posts?

4. Who walked up and down?

5. Who climbed up a tree?

6. Who raced around the trees?

7. Who said, "Guess we'll never know"?

8. Who said, "It can't disappear"?

9. Who said, "It'll be all right"?

10. Who looked down from a tree?

11. Who searched near the brook's edge?

12. Who looked through fallen leaves?

Name _____ **Date** _____

(See directions on page 139.)

Drawing Positions

Directions: Listen carefully and follow directions.

 bug under chair	 bird over cloud
stars around moon	 baseball in hand
another mouse down in corner	hat on head
 cat far away from cow	 flower near duck
  dog between boys	potato next to carrot

Name _____ Date _____

What Goes There?

Directions: In each box, draw something that might go there.

through

on top of

under

over

inside

next to

between

around

Name _____   **Date** _____

Order Please

Directions: Look at the three pictures in each row. Write 1 in the box for what happens first. Write 2 for what happens next. Write 3 for what happens last.

Name _____   **Date** _____

Where Is the Teacher's Hat?

Directions: Read each word. Then, cut out the hats found at the bottom of the page. Glue a hat to show the meaning of each word.

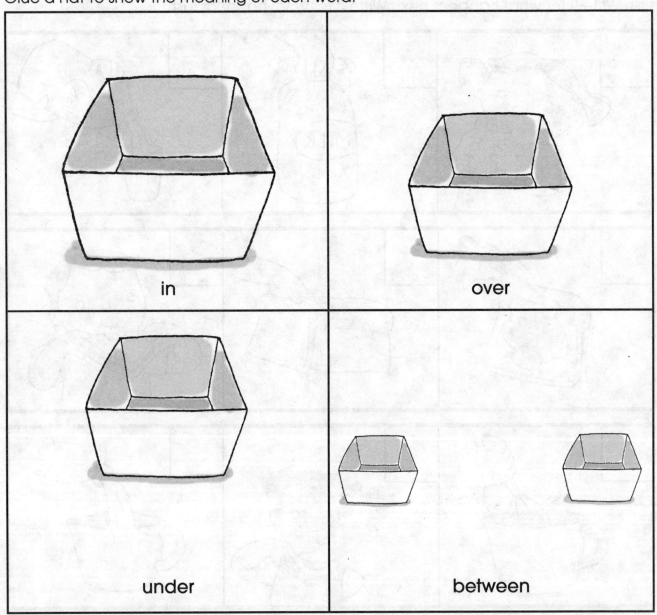

in   over

under   between

Name _____ **Date** _____

(See directions on page 140.)

Cut and Paste in Place

Directions: Listen carefully and follow directions.

(See directions on pages 135, 138, and 140.)

Position Word Cards

around	between
down	far
in	near
next to	off
on	out
over	through
under	up

Chapter 7—Alphabet
(Teacher's Guide)

Learning Center: Setting the Stage for the Pullout Story "The Name Game"
Need: tables or shelves for displays, self-stick notes, fine-tip black marker

Directions: Celebrate letters with an ABC zoo learning center. Place a table in front of the ABC Zoo bulletin board. (See directions below.) Invite students to bring stuffed animals and animal picture books, make animal drawings, etc. Write the first letter of each animal's name on a self-stick note and attach it to the animal in the center.

Bulletin Board: ABC Zoo
Need: bulletin board, roll of white paper, 12" x 18" (30.48 cm x 45.72 cm) colorful construction paper including black, 4" to 6" (10 cm to 15 cm) letter patterns, wide-tip black marker, pencils, crayons, markers, scissors, stapler or tape

Getting Ready: Cover a bulletin board or wall with white paper. Trace letter patterns on black paper and cut them out to make the title. Center the title at the top of the board. Then, with a wide-tip black marker, print each student's first name on the bulletin board.

Directions: On construction paper, have each student draw a picture of an animal that begins with the same letter as the student's name. They may use crayons or markers to give their animals spots, stripes, or other markings. Cut out the animals and attach each to the board next to the appropriate student's name.

Follow-Up: Hold a discussion comparing beginning sounds of the student and animal names displayed on the board.

Field Trip Ideas: Safaris
Visit any place where animals are found so that students may identify the first letter of each animal's name.

☐ pet store or zoo   ☐ department store stuffed animal aisle   ☐ woods or park

Companion Book: *The Jazzy Alphabet*
". . . and boogie-woogie B, bebop a boogaloo. Bim-bam blues!"

Need: *The Jazzy Alphabet* by Sherry Shahan (Philomel Books)

Directions: Before reading the Brainy Bunch story, "The Name Game," share the companion book. The rock-and-roll story is like a little tune that emphasizes the letter sounds. Each colorful collage illustration contains more objects that begin with the featured letter, making the book a fun puzzle, too.

Other Good Books to Share:
☐ *My Beastie Book of ABC* by David Frampton (HarperCollins)
☐ *Z Is for Zookeeper: A Zoo Alphabet* by Marie and Roland Smith (Sleeping Bear Press)
☐ *Zoopa: An Animal Alphabet* by Gianna Marino (Chronicle Books)

Presenting the Pullout Story: "The Name Game"

Need: "The Name Game" story (pages 167–178), 12" x 18" (30.48 cm x 45.72 cm) white construction paper, crayons, markers

Directions: Read aloud "The Name Game." Then, help each student name an animal that begins with the same first letter as the student's name. Have students draw pictures of their animals and help them print the animals' names on the pictures.

Follow-Up: Compile all of the animal drawings into a class book and place it in the ABC zoo learning center.

Music: Sing the Alphabet

Getting Ready: Display an alphabet chart or use patterns to cut out upper- and lowercase letters. Attach the letters around the walls of the classroom—the bigger the better!

Directions: Most children have heard "The Alphabet Song" sung to the tune of "Twinkle, Twinkle, Little Star." Using a pointer to indicate which letter to sing, practice singing the lyrics from start to finish. Sing "The Alphabet Song" every day.

A, B, C, D, E, F, G,   *W, X,*
H, I, J, K, L, M, N, O, P,   *Y, and Z*
Q, R, S,   *Now I know my ABCs.*
T, U, V,   *Aren't you very proud of me?*

Listening Skills: Name an Animal

Directions: Before rereading "The Name Game," tell students to listen for the children's and animals' names in the story that begin with the first letter of their own names. Read the story; then, one at a time, print each student's first name on the board. Ask each student to say the names of the child and animal in the story with the same first letter as his name. Write the names next to the student's name on the board.

Follow-Up: Ask, "Who in our class has the same beginning sound /b/ in their names?" "What animal names start with the /b/ sound?" On the board, make lists of students' and animals' names that begin with the same first sounds.

Imagination: A Trip to the Zoo

Directions: Invite students to lie back and relax. Instruct them to close their eyes and listen carefully to try to see with their imaginations the following animals at a zoo. Stress the initial sound of each animal's name. To give students time to use their visual memories and imaginations, pause at least 10 seconds after each description.

1. three pandas—*p* for pandas (pause)
2. two snakes—*s* for snakes (pause)
3. five lions in a cage—*l* for lions (pause)
4. ants on the sidewalk—*a* for ants (pause)
5. a kangaroo—*k* for kangaroo (pause)
6. two tigers—*t* for tigers (pause)
7. five frogs—*f* for frogs (pause)
8. six cows—*c* for cows (pause)
9. two white horses—*h* for horses (pause)
10. a green gorilla—*g* for gorilla (pause)
11. two red monkeys—*m* for monkeys (pause)
12. an orange ostrich—*o* for ostrich (pause)
13. two blue bobcats—*b* for bobcats (pause)
14. a pink elephant—*e* for elephant (pause)
15. four brown donkeys—*d* for donkeys (pause)
16. two red roosters—*r* for roosters (pause)
17. a white walrus—*w* for walrus (pause)
18. three striped zebras—*z* for zebras (pause)
19. two yellow yaks—*y* for yaks (pause)
20. jellyfish in the sea—*j* for jellyfish (pause)

Listening Skills: Give Them a Thumbs-Up!

Directions: Gather students on the floor around you. Explain that you will name pairs of words—an animal and a person's name. If the animal and the name begin with the same sound, students should give a thumbs-up. Thumbs-down means the words have different beginning sounds.

1. ants, Annie
2. porcupine, Bob
3. katydid, Kate
4. magpie, Maggie
5. platypus, Newton
6. snake, Yuuto
7. otter, Otto
8. eel, Eli
9. cat, David
10. gopher, Goldie
11. llama, Lana
12. fish, Ula
13. worm, Robin
14. hamster, Hannah
15. iguana, Iggy
16. dodo, Jada
17. newt, Newton
18. toad, Timmy
19. yak, Zoe
20. quail, Quentin

Listening Skills: Long Vowel Sounds

Getting Ready: List the vowels A, E, I, O, and U on the board.

Directions: One at a time, say the long vowel sounds as you point to the letters, beginning with A. Explain that students should listen carefully as you read the story. Each time students hear a long A sound, they should clap once. As you read, list each long A word on the board as students identify the sound. (Note that the long vowel sounds students hear will be spelled in a variety of ways.) Repeat with long E, long I, and so on.

Long A words: made, game, name, named, take, gray, Jada's, Kate's, katydid, quail, X-ray

Long E words: teacher, each, Annie, Cathy's, Fancy, Dotty, Eli, eel, feel, Fifi, Goldie, Iggy's, green, Japanese, beetle, katydid, Maggie's, feeling, Pilar's, Seaton's, seal, Xerxes', Zoe's, zebra, behind

Long I words: find, like, died, inside, Eli, fly, quite, high, life-sized, magpie, ride, behind

Long O words: dodo, don't, know, no, photo, ago, bowl, Goldie, gopher, over, Otto's, toad, vole, Yuuto's, Zoe's

Long U words: Ula's, unicorn, Yuuto's, costume

Critical Thinking: Name That Animal

Directions: Gather students on the floor around you. Explain that you will give three clues about an animal in the story. When they think they know what animal you are describing, students should raise their hands. After giving all three of the clues for each animal, ask someone with a raised hand to name it.

Clue 1	Clue 2	Clue 3
1. is black and white	begins with letter z	Zoe dressed up like one. (zebra)
2. has a long neck	begins with letter l	Lana brought a stuffed one. (llama)
3. is a kind of bird	begins with letter m	Maggie brought one. (magpie)
4. is good at jumping	begins with letter t	It wiggled when Timmy held it. (toad)
5. squirmed in some grass	begins with letter w	Warner brought one. (worm)
6. is an extinct bird	begins with letter d	Dotty drew one. (dodo)
7. lives in water	begins with letter e	Eli had a rubber one. (eel)
8. builds hills	begins with letter a	Annie had a jarful. (ants)
9. is a pet that lives in a bowl	begins with letter f	Fifi brought a bowl of them. (fish)
10. has a bill	begins with letter p	Pilar brought a plastic one. (platypus)
11. flies at night	begins with letter b	Babs had a model of one. (bat)
12. is a common pet	begins with letter c	Cathy's was named Fancy Pants. (cat)
13. lives underground	begins with letter g	Goldie had one. (gopher)
14. is an insect	begins with letter k	Kate brought this. (katydid)
15. was feeling ill	begins with letter n	Newton's pet was this. (newt)

Outdoor Adventure: Animals That Start Like My Name

Getting Ready: Weather permitting, go outside to play this game. Have students sit in a circle.

How to Play: Choose a student to begin. The first student says, "My name is . . . An animal that begins with the same letter as my name is . . ." and names the animal. The second player does the same and also repeats the first player's name and animal, for example, "My name is Dakota. An animal that begins like my name is dog, and an animal that begins like Fred's name is frog." The third player then names an animal and must name the second and first players' names and animals. Continue around the circle, adding to the list of name and animal pairs. If a player has difficulty remembering a classmate's animal, that person may name it for him.

Music: Sing the Consonant Song

Directions: Sing the song below to the tune of "Let Everyone Clap Hands." Begin by singing "Let everyone sing *B* like me." Students respond by singing the sound the consonant makes: "/b/ /b/." While singing the song's chorus, point to a child who will then choose a new consonant and lead the next verse. Sing all of the consonant sounds in this fashion.

Leader:	**Leader:**	**Everyone:**
Let everyone sing B *like me.*	*Let everyone sing* B *like me.*	*Come on, join our little game.*
Students:	**Students:**	*You'll find that it's*
/b/ /b/	*/b/ /b/*	*never the same.*

Visual Memory: Flash Cards

Need: Animal Picture-and-Word Cards reproducibles (pages 185 and 186), sturdy paper, paper cutter, rubber bands, glue

Getting Ready: Reproduce on sturdy paper a set of animal picture-and-word cards for each student. Use a paper cutter to cut apart the cards on the solid lines and secure each set with a rubber band.

Directions: Have students fold each card in half along the dashed line so that the word and picture are on opposite sides and then glue the backs together. Working in pairs and with two sets of cards, students should take turns holding up an animal picture while the student's partner finds the matching word. Students may flip one card over to check the answer.

Craft: Animal Parade Mural

Need: hallway or other long wall, roll of pastel colored paper, black construction paper, 4" to 6" (10 cm to 15 cm) letter patterns, wide-tip black marker, pencils, paints, scissors, stapler or tape

Getting Ready: Cover the wall with pastel colored paper. Trace letter patterns on black paper and cut them out to make the title. Center the title at the top of the mural.

Directions: Culminate the alphabet unit by having students create an animal mural with every animal they can think of. Can they include at least one animal for every letter of the alphabet? When the mural is complete, use a wide-tip black marker to print the name of each animal next to its picture.

Directions for Reproducible Activity Pages

Critical Thinking: Cut and Paste Alphabet—Page 179

Need: Cut and Paste Alphabet reproducible (page 179), scissors, glue sticks, pencils, crayons

Directions: Reread "The Name Game." Pass out page 179 and read the directions aloud. Let students work independently to glue the beginning sound to the matching alphabet picture. Encourage them to color the pictures.

Follow-Up: After students have completed the worksheets, have them name their favorite *c*, *d*, and *s* animals and draw them on the backs of their papers.

Language: The Teacher's Name Game—Page 180

Need: The Teacher's Name Game reproducible (page 180), pencils

Directions: Reread "The Name Game." This time as you read, stress the beginning sounds of the character's names and their animals. Print each name and animal pair on the board and encourage students to say the words together. Circle all of the beginning and subsequent letters that are the same in each pair of words. Count them. Pass out page 180. Have students work with partners to complete the worksheet. Ask students "Who won the name game?"

Story Recall: Matching—Page 181

Need: Matching reproducible (page 181), pencils

Directions: Reread "The Name Game." Ask students to listen carefully to remember which animal each character in the story brought. Pass out page 181. Read the 12 students' names together and discuss each animal. Have students work independently to draw lines connecting each animal picture with the correct student's name.

Visual Memory: At the Beginning—Page 182

Need: At the Beginning reproducible (page 182), pencils

Directions: Pass out page 182. Have students take turns naming the animals. Make the initial sound of each animal's name. Point to the correct letters on an alphabet chart as students fill in the blanks.

Fine Motor: I Can Print the Alphabet—Page 183

Need: I Can Print the Alphabet reproducible (page 183), pencils, crayons

Directions: Pass out page 183. Read aloud the letters. Make sure students understand they should use a crayon to trace each upper- and lowercase letter and then print each letter again with a pencil.

Critical Thinking: Take Your Pick—Page 184

Need: Take Your Pick reproducible (page 184), scissors, glue sticks, pencils, crayons

Directions: Pass out page 184 and read aloud the directions. Help students find the names for their six favorites of the animals listed. Then, have students cut along the dashed lines to cut out the names. Allow time for students to complete the worksheets independently.

Follow-Up: In large group setting, invite students to discuss the animals they chose as favorites and share their drawings.

Game: Animal Flash Cards—Pages 185 and 186

Need: Animal Picture-and-Word Cards reproducibles (pages 185 and 186), sturdy paper, paper cutter

Getting Ready: Reproduce on sturdy paper a set of animal picture-and word-cards for each student. Use a paper cutter to cut apart the cards on the solid lines.

Directions: Have students fold each card in half along the dashed line and glue the backs together to create sets of flash cards. Students may work in pairs, using the cards to test each other for naming the animals, naming the first letter of the animal names, or reading the animal words.

Directions for Reproducible Activity Pages, CONTINUED

Game: Animal Concentration—Pages 185 and 186

Need: Animal Picture-and-Word Cards reproducibles (pages 185 and 186), sturdy paper, paper cutter

Getting Ready: Reproduce on sturdy paper one set of animal picture-and-word cards for each group of two to four players. Cut along both the solid and dashed lines to make 52 separate animal picture cards and animal word cards. Discard the wild cards.

How to Play:
1. Place the 52 cards facedown in rows. You may place pictures and words in separate groups.
2. Players take turns flipping over pairs of cards to try to match an animal picture with its name.
3. When a player makes a match, he keeps those two cards.
4. If a player turns over two cards that are not a match, he places them facedown again.
5. When all of the cards have been collected, the player with the most matched pairs wins.

Game: Animal Rummy—Pages 185 and 186

Need: Animal Picture-and-Word Cards reproducibles (pages 185 and 186), sturdy paper, paper cutter

Getting Ready: Reproduce on sturdy paper two sets of animal picture-and-word cards for each group of two to four players. Cut along both the solid and dashed lines to make two cards of each animal picture and two cards of each animal word, plus four wild cards.

How to Play:
1. Shuffle the cards and deal eight cards to each player. The remaining cards are stacked facedown. Players look in their hands for sets of four matching cards (two each of both pictures and words). If a set of four cards is found, the player places them faceup.
2. Players take turns drawing the top card from the deck (or the last card discarded faceup by the previous player) and discarding a card.
3. After all of the cards have been drawn, shuffle the discard pile, turn the cards facedown, and continue to play.
4. The first player to make two complete sets of four matching cards wins.

Game: Animal Picture BINGO—Pages 185 and 186

Need: BINGO reproducible (page 30), Animal Picture-and-Word Cards reproducibles (pages 185 and 186), colorful sturdy paper, paper cutter, scissors, glue sticks

Getting Ready:
1. Reproduce a blank BINGO card and a set of animal picture-and-word cards for each student.
2. Cut the sturdy paper into 1.5" x 1.5" (4 cm x 4 cm) paper chips to cover the BINGO squares.
3. Pass out a set of the animal picture-and-word cards, a BINGO card, and 25 paper chips to each student.
4. Have students cut along dashed lines to cut apart the picture cards and word cards.
5. Next, have each student choose 24 of the 26 animal pictures. Students should discard the two extra pictures and the wild cards but save the animal word cards for the follow-up game below.
6. Students should trim the animal pictures to fit on the BINGO squares and then paste them on the BINGO cards. Allow plenty of time for this step.

How to Play:
1. Say "*B*" and name one of the 26 animals.
2. Students should look under *B* for a picture of that animal, and if found, cover it with a paper chip.
3. Next, say "*I*" and name another animal. Students look under *I* for that animal and cover it.
4. Repeat, working across the card with the letters *N*, *G*, and *O*. Then, start over with *B*.
5. The first player to cover five squares in a row horizontally, vertically, or diagonally calls "BINGO!" and wins the game.

Follow-Up: Play the same game using animal words instead of pictures on the BINGO cards.

The Name Game

ABC

To learn the sounds of letters all,
The teacher made a little game.

"Each of you find an animal
That starts just like your name."

Annie had a jar of ants.
Babs brought in a model bat.

Cathy's cat, named Fancy Pants,
Wore a shirt and flowered hat.

Dotty drew a clumsy dodo,   No one now can take a photo
Like a penguin, don't you know?   Since it died out long ago.

From inside his canvas pack,   He passed it around the class and back
Eli took a rubber eel.   For everyone to touch and feel.

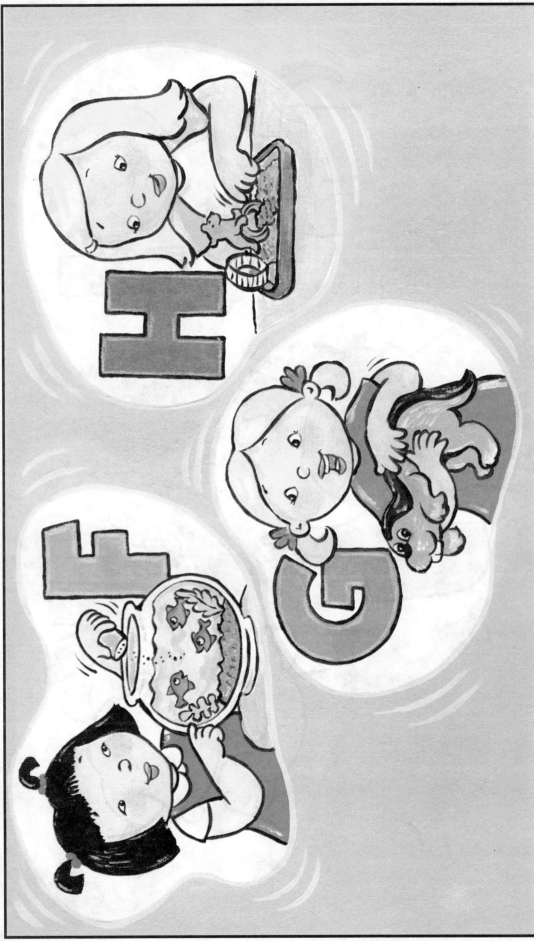

Fifi brought a bowl of fish.
Goldie held a gray-brown gopher.

Hannah's hamster had a dish
Of food that it kept turning over.

171

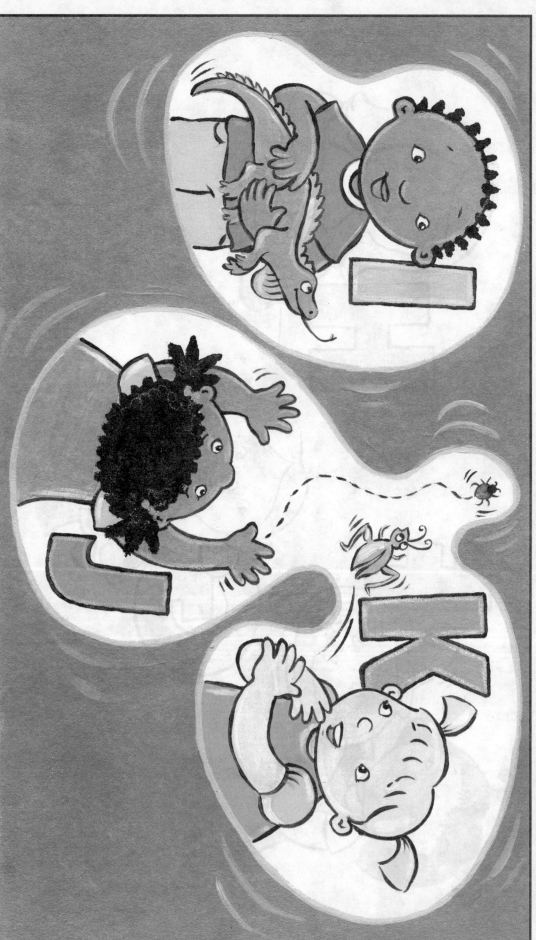

Iggy's green iguana's stare
Made Jada's Japanese beetle fly.

Kate's katydid jumped up, too;
They really were quite high.

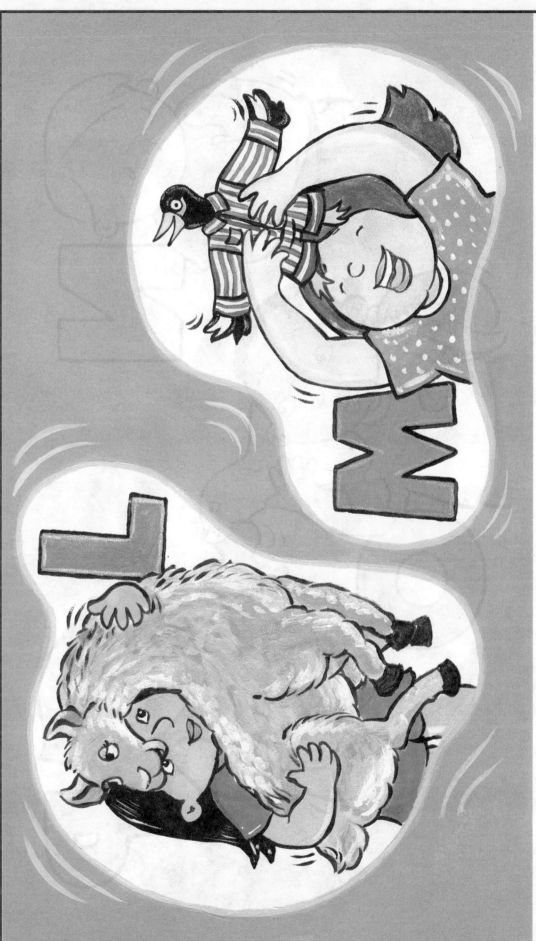

Lana's life-sized, limp-necked llama

Maggie's magpie wore pajamas

Lost some stuffing—what a wreck!

From its claws up to its neck.

Newton's newt was feeling ill
From its ride upon the bus.

Otto's otter nipped the bill
Of Pilar's plastic platypus.

Quentin's quail had seven eggs
That soon would hatch as
little chicks.

Robin's robin stretched its legs
And scratched around its
nest of twigs.

The Brainy Bunch Kids—Learning the Basics

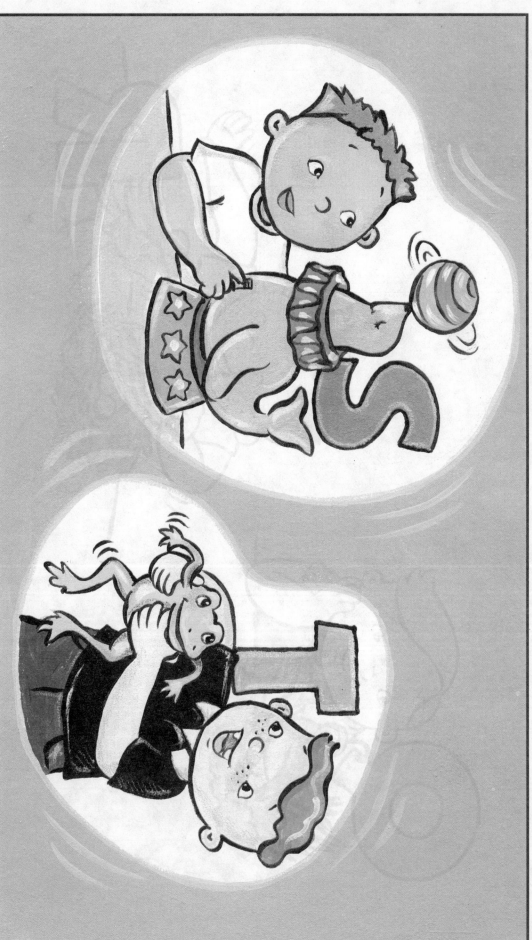

Seaton's seal, fat as a hog,
Wowed the class with all
its tricks.

Timmy brought along his toad
Full of wiggles, warts, and kicks.

Ula's unicorn was glass;
Velma's vole, a ball of fur.

Warner's worm squirmed in some grass.
Xerxes's X-ray fish were blurred.

177

Yuuto's and Zoe's costume split,
A zebra front, behind a yak.

In the zebra, Zoe fit.
Yuuto hung out in the back.

KE-804011 © Key Education

Name _____ **Date** _____

Cut and Paste Alphabet

Directions: Cut out the letters below on the dashed lines. Glue each letter in the correct box to match the animal and its beginning sound.

Name _____ Date _____

The Teacher's Name Game

Directions: Look at each pair of words. How many beginning letters are the same? Circle them. Count them. Write the number in the box. The first one has been done for you.

1. Annie ants	**2**	14. Newton newt	
2. Babs bat		15. Otto otter	
3. Cathy cat		16. Pilar platypus	
4. Dotty dodo		17. Quentin quail	
5. Eli eel		18. Robin robin	
6. Fifi fish		19. Seaton seal	
7. Goldie gopher		20. Timmy toad	
8. Hannah hamster		21. Ula unicorn	
9. Iggy iguana		22. Velma vole	
10. Jada Japanese		23. Warner worm	
11. Kate katydid		24. Xerxes X-ray fish	
12. Lana llama		25. Yuuto yak	
13. Maggie magpie		26. Zoe zebra	

Name _____ Date _____

Matching

Directions: Draw a line to match each animal with the student who brought it.

A.

B.

C.

D.

E.

F.

G.

H.

I.

J.

K.

L.

1. Warner

2. Seaton

3. Annie

4. Babs

5. Zoe

6. Cathy

7. Quentin

8. Fifi

9. Pilar

10. Iggy

11. Robin

12. Dotty

Name _____ **Date** _____

(See directions on page 165.) # At the Beginning

Directions: Listen carefully and follow directions. Write the first letter of each animal's name in the blank.

 _____apanese beetle

 _____at

 _____nicorn

 _____tter

 _____ebra

 _____ewt

 _____latypus

 _____amster

 _____guana

 _____eal

 _____uail

 _____obin

 _____at

 _____ole

 _____opher

 _____ish

 _____nt

 _____agpie

 _____orm

 _____oad

 _____odo

 _____atydid

 _____-ray fish

 _____ak

Name _____ **Date** _____

I Can Print the Alphabet

Directions: Trace each letter with a crayon. Then, use a pencil to print letter again.

Aa   Bb   Cc

Dd   Ee   Ff

Gg   Hh   Ii

Jj   Kk   Ll

Mm   Nn   Oo

Pp   Qq   Rr

Ss   Tt   Uu

Vv   Ww   Xx

Yy   Zz

Name _____ **Date** _____

Take Your Pick

Directions: Read the animal names below. Find the names of your six favorite animals. Cut out the six names on the dashed lines. Glue each name in a box. Draw a picture of each animal.

ant	bat	cat	dodo	eel	fish
gopher	hamster	iguana	Japanese beetle	katydid
llama	magpie	newt	otter	platypus
quail	robin	seal	toad	unicorn
vole	worm	X-ray fish	yak	zebra

Animal Picture-and-Word Cards

(Cut apart on solid lines for combined picture-and-word cards. Cut apart on both solid and dashed lines for separate picture and word cards. See game directions on pages 164–166.)

	ant		bat
	cat		dodo
	eel		fish
	gopher		hamster
	iguana		Japanese beetle
	katydid		llama
	magpie		newt

Animal Picture-and-Word Cards

(Cut apart on solid lines for combined picture-and-word cards. Cut apart on both solid and dashed lines for separate picture and word cards. See game directions on pages 164–166.)

picture	word	picture	word
	otter		platypus
	quail		robin
	seal		toad
	unicorn		vole
	worm		X-ray fish
	yak		zebra
Wild!	*Wild!*	*wild!*	*wild!*

Chapter 8—Feelings
(Teacher's Guide)

Learning Center: Setting the Stage for the Pullout Story "Rude Ruby"

Need: Good Manners Recognition reproducible (page 211), Award Certificate reproducible (page 212), pencils, scissors, small cardboard box with lid, comfortable gathering area

Getting Ready: Reproduce a stack of good manners acknowledgment slips and cut them apart. Cut a slit in the lid of the box. Place the slips, pencils, and the box in the gathering area.

Directions: To reinforce good citizenship and positive self-images, set aside time each day to acknowledge good manners. Introduce the center by placing some of your own acknowledgements of good manners in the box, for example, "Presented to Sarah for holding open the outside door." Let students know that their slips may be submitted either signed or unsigned. Since filling out the slips may prove too difficult for many children, be available to help or enlist aids and older students to act as scribes. When completed, all of the slips go into the box. Be aware of students who rarely receive recognition from classmates; you may wish to continue to add your own slips to the box throughout the unit. Gather students around you. With great fanfare, one at a time, pull out the good manners acknowledgement slips and read them aloud. Culminate this activity by passing out a few award certificates.

Bulletin Board: Our Class Rules

Need: bulletin board, roll of white paper, black construction paper, 4" to 6" (10 cm to 15 cm) letter patterns, wide-tip black marker, crayons, markers, paints, scissors, stapler or tape

Getting Ready: Cover a bulletin board or wall with white paper. Trace letter patterns on black paper and cut them out to make the title. Center the title at the top of the board.

Directions: Ask students to help you come up with a list of class rules. Begin by having them discuss ways to show good manners. With a wide-tip black marker, print their ideas on the bulletin board. Allow time for students to decorate the board by illustrating the rules with crayons, markers, or paints.

Presenting the Pullout Story: "Rude Ruby"

Need: "Rude Ruby" story (pages 195–206)

Directions: Read aloud the story. Follow with a class discussion about being "the new kid." Lead the discussion toward reasons why Ruby might have been rude. Print students' ideas on the board, for example, Ruby was afraid, she had not been taught how to behave properly, she was acting out ways she was treated at home, etc. Culminate with a discussion of ways people compensate in uncomfortable situations.

Companion Book: *The Recess Queen*

"If kids ever crossed her, she'd push 'em and smoosh 'em,
lollapaloosh 'em, hammer 'em, slammer 'em, kitz and kajammer 'em."

Need: *The Recess Queen* by Alexis O'Neill (Scholastic Press)

Directions: After reading "Rude Ruby," share the companion book. Have students name ways Ruby and Mean Jean are alike. For example, both Jean and Ruby push through other people so that they can be first.

Other Good Books to Share:
- *Excuse Me!* by Lisa Kopelke (Simon & Schuster Books for Young Readers)
- *Best Best Friends* by Margaret Chodos-Irvine (Harcourt)
- *This Little Piggy's Book of Manners* by Kathryn Madeline Allen (Henry Holt)
- *Madeline and the Bad Hat* by Ludwig Bemelmans (Viking)
- *Grody's Not So Golden Rules* by Nicole Rubel (Harcourt)
- *Meet Wild Boars* by Meg Rosoff and Sophie Blackall (Henry Holt)
- *What Are You So Grumpy About?* by Tom Lichtenheld (Little, Brown & Co.)

Discussion: How Was Ruby Rude?

Directions: Talk about specific ways Ruby was rude. List them on the board. Be sure to avoid finger-pointing and discussions about classmates who may act out. After making the list of Ruby's bad manners, discuss each one and record an action that would be the opposite behavior.

Bad Manners	Good Manners
1. Ruby wasn't considerate of others' feelings.	Be considerate.
2. Ruby didn't take turns.	Take turns.
3. Ruby criticized others.	Encourage others.
4. Ruby stuck out her tongue.	Smile and be cheerful.
5. Ruby copied.	Do your own work.
6. Ruby didn't follow the rules of the game.	Play fair.
7. Ruby didn't know why others didn't like her.	Be self-aware.

Follow-Up: Compare the list of good behaviors that are the opposite of Ruby's actions with the rules on "Our Class Rules" bulletin board (page 187).

Imagination: That Feeling!

Directions: Gather students around you. Instruct them to close their eyes and listen carefully to try to see with their imaginations the situations you will describe. To give students time to use their visual memories and imaginations, pause at least 20 seconds after each description.

1. You find a lost dog and return it to its rightful owner. (pause)
2. You win the spelling bee at school. (pause)
3. You lose your lunch money. At recess, someone finds it and gives it back to you. (pause)
4. You are playing with your friend's favorite toy and accidentally break it. (pause)
5. You see an elderly woman drop a five-dollar bill. You pick it up, run after her, and give it back. (pause)
6. Someone gives you a cute puppy, and your parents let you keep it. (pause)
7. You stay up late watching TV. The next day at school, you feel sleepy and grumpy. (pause)
8. You're playing baseball in your yard. You hit a ball, and it crashes through a window. (pause)
9. It is night. You are alone in your room. You hear strange noises in your backyard. (pause)
10. Your mother gives you a surprise birthday party, and all of your friends are there. (pause)

Drama: What to Do about Ruby

Directions: Gather students on the floor around you. Reread "Rude Ruby." Then, divide students into pairs. Have students choose the part of Zoe, Jada, Eli, or Yuuto. Each pair of students will make up a skit called "What to Do about Ruby." Allow plenty of time for each pair to create a short play about how to deal with Ruby and then rehearse it. As needed, you play the character of Rude Ruby as students perform their skits for the class.

Follow-Up: After the performances, discuss the varied approaches for dealing with Ruby. Which plan do students think will be most successful?

Craft: Paper Plate Puppets

Need: paper plates, craft sticks, tape, markers

Getting Ready: Print a list of feelings on the board: *happy, sad, proud, confused, afraid, worried, cross, surprised,* and *disappointed.* Read the list to students.

Directions: Have each student choose one of the feelings. On the front of a paper plate, each student should use markers to draw facial features indicating the chosen feeling. Tape a craft stick to the back of each plate. Have each student take a turn holding her paper-plate puppet in front of her face and telling about a time when she experienced that feeling, for example, "I felt happy the day . . ."

Music: Such a Good Feeling

Getting Ready: Once again, visit Mr. Rogers' Neighborhood. Go online to http://pbskids.org/rogers/songlist/ to find words to the following songs.

"It's Such a Good Feeling"
"This Is Just the Day"
"There Are Many Ways"

Directions: After students hear Fred Rogers sing each of the songs, teach them the words. Sing the songs often so that students will memorize them and have them hidden in their hearts.

Discussion: Let Me Count the Ways

Directions: Hold a discussion about other ways to show good manners at home besides saying "please" and "thank you." One at a time, list on the board the following ways to show good manners. Have students give specific examples of how they can demonstrate each.

Good Manners	Examples
1. Respect the home you live in.	Keep my own room clean.
2. Be helpful and cooperative.	Set the table without being asked.
3. Listen.	Pay attention when my mom gives me a direction.
4. Share.	Let my brother ride my bike.
5. Observe home rules.	Go to bed on time without complaining.
6. Be self-disciplined.	Do my chores before playing outside.
7. Speak in appropriate ways.	Don't yell when I'm mad.
8. Be honest.	Tell the truth if I did something wrong.
9. Be fair.	Don't cheat when we play games.
10. Be kind and loving.	Help my little sister put on her shoes.

Field Trip Ideas: Putting Good Manners to Work

Getting Ready: Visiting a nursing home or senior center will give students an opportunity to be polite to strangers. Ahead of time, have students practice introducing themselves and shaking hands as a greeting. Practice a song or prepare a choral reading for the seniors. (See below.) Also, discuss questions that students might ask the seniors they are visiting.

1. When you went to school, what were some of your school's rules?
2. When you were my age, was there a bully in your school? Tell me about it.
3. Do you think children have better manners or worse manners now than when you were a child? Why?

Directions: When you arrive at the center, pair students with seniors. Allow time for students to greet and talk with their partners. Culminate with the Ruby Choral Reading or song (below).

Game: Feelings Rummy

Need: Color the Feelings reproducible (page 209), card stock, paper cutter, rubber bands

Getting Ready: For each pair of students, reproduce page 209 four times. Cut apart the cards on the solid lines and secure each deck of 32 cards with a rubber band.

Directions: Play Feelings Rummy. Divide students into pairs. One player should shuffle the deck and deal eight cards apiece. Players take turns drawing and discarding a card to try to get two sets of four matching cards to win.

Drama: Ruby Choral Reading

Need: Ruby Choral Reading (pages 190–192)

Getting Ready: Reproduce the reading on pages 190–192 for each student.

Directions: Assign parts. You or a student or students who can read might be Voice #1, reading the first line of each verse. Those who cannot read or memorize lines should be assigned the second and third lines of each verse, which simply echo the first line. The fourth line might be a chorus (including you) or a solo by Voice #1. Practice the reading to the rhythm of "Mary Had a Little Lamb." When students are familiar with the reading, perform it for parents or at a senior center.

Ruby Choral Reading

(read with the rhythm or sung to the tune of "Mary Had a Little Lamb")

Voice #1: ..... Ruby was the new girl's name,
Group: ..... New girl's name, new girl's name.
Ruby was the new girl's name.
Voice #1/Chorus: ..... She wore a big, wide grin.

Voice #1: ..... The Brainies tried to welcome her,
Group: ..... Welcome her, welcome her.
The Brainies tried to welcome her
Voice #1/Chorus: ..... To help her fit right in.

Voice #1: ..... At lunchtime, Zoe asked her,
Group: ..... Asked her, asked her.
At lunchtime, Zoe asked her
Voice #1/Chorus: ..... To come and sit with them.

Voice #1: ..... Ruby answered, "That's a laugh.
Group: ..... That's a laugh. That's a laugh."
Ruby answered, "That's a laugh.
Voice #1/Chorus: ..... I choose my own friends."

Voice #1: ..... The basic rules of manners,
Group: ..... Of manners, of manners,
The basic rules of manners,
Voice #1/Chorus: ..... She could not seem to learn.

Voice #1: ..... When she wished to speak in class,
Group: ..... Speak in class, speak in class,
When she wished to speak in class,
Voice #1/Chorus: ..... She would not wait her turn.

Voice #1: ..... She criticized her classmates,
Group: ..... Her classmates, her classmates.
She criticized her classmates
Voice #1/Chorus: ..... In most things that she said.

Voice #1: ..... And when the class would form a line,
Group: ..... Form a line, form a line,
And when the class would form a line,
Voice #1/Chorus: ..... She'd elbow in ahead.

(Ruby Choral Reading, continued)

Voice #1: ......She copied Yuuto's spelling test,
Group: ......Spelling test, spelling test.
She copied Yuuto's spelling test
Voice #1/Chorus: ......And got the answers right

Voice #1: ......And from the back, stuck out her tongue,
Group: ......Out her tongue, out her tongue,
And from the back, stuck out her tongue
Voice #1/Chorus: ......When others would recite.

Voice #1: ......At recess, they played dodgeball,
Group: ......Played dodgeball, played dodgeball.
At recess, they played dodgeball.
Voice #1/Chorus: ......She laughed and looked around

Voice #1: ......When she hit Eli in the head,
Group: ......In the head, in the head,
When she hit Eli in the head
Voice #1/Chorus: ......And knocked him to the ground.

Voice #1: ......Valentine's Day was coming,
Group: ......Was coming, was coming.
Valentine's Day was coming,
Voice #1/Chorus: ......And Eli said with scorn,

Voice #1: ......"Ruby's getting nothing,
Group: ......Nothing, nothing.
Ruby's getting nothing,
Voice #1/Chorus: ......As sure as I was born.

Voice #1: ......"She's never ever friendly,
Group: ......Friendly, friendly.
She's never ever friendly.
Voice #1/Chorus: ......She treats us all like dirt.

Voice #1: ......"We've all been waiting for this day,
Group: ...... For this day, for this day.
We've all been waiting for this day;
Voice #1/Chorus: ......It's time for her to hurt."

(Ruby Choral Reading, continued)

Voice #1: ...... Jada said, "Now, Eli,

Group: ...... Now, Eli, now, Eli,"

Jada said, "Now, Eli,

Voice #1/Chorus: ...... There's much in what you say.

Voice #1: ...... "But before we are unkind,

Group: ...... Are unkind, are unkind,

But before we are unkind,

Voice #1/Chorus: ...... Let's try a better way."

Voice #1: ...... Ruby got no valentines,

Group: ...... Valentines, valentines.

Ruby got no valentines,

Voice #1/Chorus: ...... So she sat and cried.

Voice #1: ...... "No one seems to like me,

Group: ...... To like me, to like me.

No one seems to like me.

Voice #1/Chorus: ...... I really don't know why."

Voice #1: ...... The Brainies sat beside her,

Group: ...... Beside her, beside her.

The Brainies sat beside her

Voice #1/Chorus: ...... And handed her a card.

Voice #1: ...... All four of them had signed it,

Group: ...... Had signed it, had signed it.

All four of them had signed it,

Voice #1/Chorus: ...... Their names on small white hearts.

Voice #1: ...... It may seem like a gamble,

Group: ...... A gamble, a gamble.

It may seem like a gamble,

Voice #1/Chorus: ...... But mostly, it is true:

Voice #1: ...... Be a friend to others,

Group: ...... To others, to others.

Be a friend to others,

Voice #1/Chorus: ...... And they'll be friends to you.

Directions for Reproducible Activity Pages

Connecting with Family: Sharing Feelings with Family—Page 207

Need: Sharing Feelings with Family reproducible (page 207), pencils

Directions: Pass out page 207 and read aloud the word in each box. Explain that students will take this page home. They should ask four people to share a story about a time when they felt one of the four feelings. After hearing each person's story, students should illustrate it in the correct box.

Follow-Up: Back in class, take time to share pictures and retell some of the stories.

Language: Cooperate!—Page 208

Need: Cooperate! reproducible (page 208), black crayons

Directions: Pair students. Give each pair a copy of page 208 and just one crayon. Explain that each pair of students must share their crayon and complete the page in only five minutes.

Follow-Up: When time is called, discuss how students were able to cooperate to finish their pages. How did it feel to have to work together? Was it hard to finish the page on time? How did students use teamwork to be successful?

Following Directions: Color the Feelings—Page 209

Need: Color the Feelings reproducible (page 209), pencils, crayons

Directions: Discuss feelings. Remind students that we do not always feel like wearing happy faces and that we have a right to all of our feelings—including sadness, anxiety, and impatience. The various expressions we show on our faces serve as good communicators. They tell those around us what we need: help, attention, affection, and so on. Pass out page 209. Discuss each face and the feeling it conveys. Read aloud each direction. Allow plenty of time for students to complete the work independently.

1. Use your pink crayon to color the face that is happy.
2. Color purple the face that shows fear.
3. Use your red crayon to circle the angry face.
4. Color the sad face blue.
5. Use your favorite color to color the face that shows pride.
6. Color the confused and frustrated face brown.
7. Use your green crayon to color the face that looks surprised.
8. Color the worried face yellow.

Follow-Up: Have students think about a time when they felt one of the feelings: happy, afraid, angry, sad, proud, confused, surprised, or worried. Then, without using the actual word for the feeling, invite them to share a short story about that time. After hearing each story, have classmates guess how the storyteller was feeling.

Directions for Reproducible Activity Pages, CONTINUED

Language: Autograph Hound—Page 210

Need: Autograph Hound reproducible (page 210), pencils

Directions: Explain that a good way for students to make new friends at school is to talk to other students with whom they don't usually talk. Pass out page 210 and explain that the worksheet is a contest. During one recess, students should collect as many autographs as they can from other students who are not in their classroom. Even though students will rush to complete the worksheet, remind them to use good manners while collecting autographs. For example, they should introduce themselves, politely explain why they need to have other students sign the page, and remember to say "please" and "thank you."

Follow-Up: Back in the classroom, count autographs to see which students collected the most. Discuss how students felt approaching other children whom they did not know. Ask, "Could this be the same feeling Ruby had the first day at her new school?" Give an award certificate (page 212) to each winner.

Connecting with Family: Good Manners Acknowledgment—Page 211

Need: Good Manners Recognition reproducible (page 211), pencils

Directions: Besides using the good manners acknowledgement slips as a class activity, have students honor the good manners of others. On separate occasions, help students fill out slips and deliver or send the slips to the appropriate people, for example, parents, siblings, older students, neighbors, school employees, or community workers.

Surprise Activity: Award Certificates—Page 212

Need: Award Certificate reproducible (page 212), paper, crayons or markers, cookies, punch

Getting Ready: Hold a class awards assembly. Begin by letting each student choose someone she wants to honor. Allow time for students to take turns telling about the people they have chosen to honor. Choose a time and day for the assembly. Make invitations for all those who will be honored and mail or deliver them. Help students fill out award certificates for their honorees.

Directions: On the day of the assembly, let each student present an award to his special person. Encourage the student to give an example of how the person is especially courteous.

Follow-Up: If possible, serve cookies and punch to all attendees.

Rude Ruby

Ruby was the new
girl's name.
She wore a big, wide grin.

The Brainies tried to
welcome her
To help her fit right in.

KE-804011 © Key Education

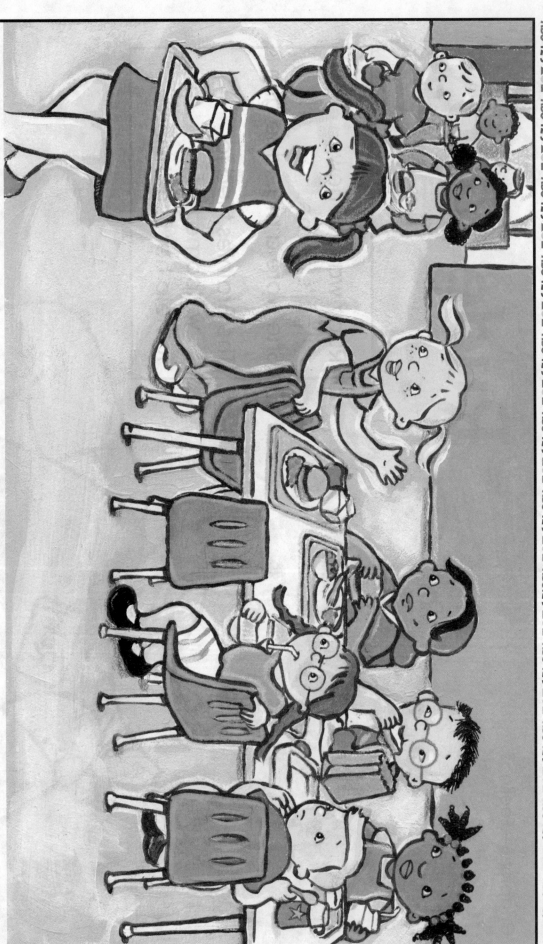

At lunchtime, Zoe asked her
To come and sit with them.

Ruby answered, "That's a laugh.
I choose my own friends."

The basic rules of manners, she could not seem to learn. When she wished to speak in class, she would not wait her turn.

The Brainy Bunch Kids—Learning the Basics

She criticized her classmates.
In most things that she said,

And when the class would form a line,
She'd elbow in ahead.

She copied Yuuto's spelling test And from the back, stuck out her tongue
And got the answers right When others would recite.

The Brainy Bunch Kids—Learning the Basics

At recess, they played dodgeball.
She laughed and looked around.
When she hit Eli in the head
And knocked him to the ground.

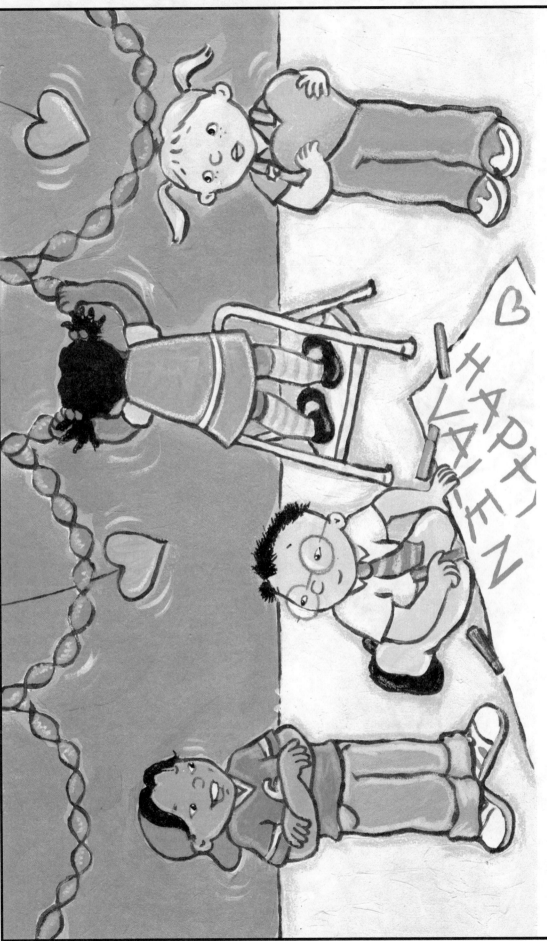

Valentine's Day was coming,
And Eli said with scorn,

"Ruby's getting nothing
As sure as I was born.

"She's never ever friendly.
She treats us all like dirt.

We've all been waiting for this day;
It's time for her to hurt.

Jada said, "Now, Eli,
There's much in what you say,

But before we are unkind,
Let's try a better way."

The Brainy Bunch Kids—Learning the Basics

Ruby got no valentines,
So she sat and cried.

"No one seems to like me.
I really don't know why."

The Brainies sat beside her
And handed her a card.

All four of them had signed it,
Their names on small white hearts.

It may seem like a gamble,   Be a friend to others,
But mostly, it is true: And they'll be friends to you.

Name _____   **Date** _____

Sharing Feelings with Family

Directions: Read the feeling words below. Ask four people to share a story about a time when they felt one of the feelings. Then, draw a picture about each story.

happy	sad
afraid	angry

Names _____ **Date** _____

Cooperate!

Directions: Read the number of spots or stripes for each animal. Work with your partner to draw them. You may use only one black crayon—not two. You will have only five minutes to work.

Name _____   **Date** _____

(See directions on pages 189 and 193.)

Color the Feelings

Directions: Listen carefully and follow directions.

Name _____ **Date** _____

Autograph Hound

Directions: Ask kids who are not in your class to sign their names on the hound.

Good Manners Recognition

Presented to

_____

A friend acknowledges you for

_____

_____

From: _____

Date: _____

Good Manners Recognition

Presented to

_____

A friend acknowledges you for

_____

_____

From: _____

Date: _____

Good Manners Recognition

Presented to

_____

A friend acknowledges you for

_____

_____

From: _____

Date: _____

Good Manners Recognition

Presented to

_____

A friend acknowledges you for

_____

_____

From: _____

Date: _____

AWARD CERTIFICATE

presented to

in recognition of

Signature:

Date:

Chapter 9—Transportation
(Teacher's Guide)

Learning Center: Setting the Stage for the Pullout Story "The Transportation Song"
Need: table for books and toy vehicles, area for playing on the floor with toy cars
Directions: Set up a learning center to celebrate transportation. The center might include:
- picture books about machines that move and haul
- toy vehicles such as Hot Wheels®, Tonka®, or Matchbox® cars and trucks
- toy garages and other buildings
- long sheet of bulletin board paper placed on the floor for drawing streets and roads to be used with toy vehicles and buildings

Companion Book: *CLINK, CLANK, CLUNK!*
"Tucka, Tucka, Tucka, Thunk,
'Who wants to ride in my hunk-o-junk?' said Rabbit."
Need: *Clink, Clank, Clunk!* by Miriam Aroner (Boyds Mills Press)
Directions: While driving to town in his car, Rabbit picks up Mole, Squirrel, Porcupine, Possum, Beaver, Crow, Skunk, Fox, and Cow. As each new friend climbs aboard, something else goes wrong with Rabbit's car. The book features a simple, rhythmic text with varied sound and action words.
Follow-Up: To reinforce listening skills, reread the book. The second time, pause after every series of car sounds so that students may repeat them.

varoom, varoom, varoom!	bang, boom! puff, puff, puff!
boing, boing, ping!	tucka, tucka, tucka, thunk
squeak, squeak, squeak!	clankety, clankety, clankety, clunk!
rumble, rumble, thump	clankety, clankety, clankety, clank!
fizzle, fizzle, hiss, hiss, hiss!	clunk! clank! rumble, thump! screech! bang! boom!
krak, krak, krak! pop, pop, pop!	beep, beep! whish, whoosh!

Other Good Books to Share:
- *Chuck's Truck* by Peggy Perry Anderson (Houghton Mifflin)
- *Good Morning, Digger* by Anne Rockwell (Viking)

Presenting the Pullout Story: "The Transportation Song"
Need: "The Transportation Song" story (pages 219–230)
Directions: Present "The Transportation Song" by singing the words of the story to the tune of "The Wheels on the Bus."

Discussion: Let's Talk Tractors
Directions: After singing "The Transportation Song" story, hold a discussion with students about transportation.
1. How did you get to school today?
2. Have you ever ridden on a tractor? In a taxi? On a train? In a boat? In an airplane?
3. Do you know someone who earns a living by driving a truck? Tractor? Taxi? Bus? Boat? Do you know someone who can fly a plane?
4. Who does most of the driving in your family? What kind of a car does your family own?
5. Do you know anyone who drives a motorcycle? A motor scooter?
6. Which is your favorite mode of transportation? Why?

Field Trip Ideas: Connecting with Transporters
Any of the following excursions will enhance your transportation unit.
- Visit a store that sells lawn tractors and mowers.
- Visit a fire, police, or ambulance station and view the vehicles.
- Visit a car or motorcycle dealership and have a salesman demonstrate a vehicle.

Bulletin Board: Transportation to School

Need: wall or bulletin board, roll of light blue paper, colorful construction paper including black, 4" to 6" (10 cm to 15 cm) letter patterns, scissors, wide-tip black marker, crayons, markers, stapler or tape

Getting Ready: Cover a wall or bulletin board with light blue paper. Trace letter patterns on black paper and cut them out to make the title. Center the title at the top of the board. Draw a long school bus with big windows on the board and outline the bus and windows with the wide-tip black marker.

Directions: Have students who ride the school bus draw self-portraits on construction paper for the bus windows. Cut out the faces and attach them inside the bus window frames. Have students who do not ride a bus draw cars, vans, trucks, etc., with their faces in the passenger windows. Cut out these vehicles and attach them around the bus. If some children walk or ride bicycles to school, have them portray these modes of transportation and display them close to the side of the board.

Discussion: Helmet Myths and Facts

Need: poster board for each group of four students, pencils, crayons, markers

Directions: Begin by asking, "How many of you wear a helmet when you ride a bike, scooter, or skateboard? Do your friends wear helmets?" Explain that a helmet is as much a part of the bicycle as the handlebars and tires. Tell students that they should never ride without one. One at a time, read aloud the three helmet myths below. Take time to let students voice their opinions about each myth. Then, present the appropriate facts.

Myth: Helmets look dumb. I don't want anyone to see me wearing one.

Fact: Helmets are designed to help prevent skull and brain injuries. A crash can cause permanent brain damage or death. Being safe and wearing a helmet doesn't look dumb; it looks smart! Plus, being seen is the point. Helmets make it easier for motorists to see the biker. If they can see you, they won't run into or over you.

Myth: Wearing a helmet is uncomfortable; it hurts my head, and it makes me too hot.

Fact: Helmets used to be uncomfortable, but new helmets are lightweight and well ventilated. Good fit is important for a helmet to be comfortable, so always try on a helmet before buying it. You can find one that will feel just right for you.

Myth: I never crash, so I don't need to wear a helmet.

Fact: Even professional bike racers can crash. Studies have shown that in three out of every four bike crashes, bikers get some sort of injury to the head. Every biker should wear a helmet.

Follow-Up: After the discussion, divide students into groups of three or four. Have them work together to make "Wear a Helmet" posters. You might want to list slogan ideas on the board.

- ❏ Look Smart! Wear a Helmet!
- ❏ Be Seen! Stay Safe!
- ❏ Helmets Are Cool!
- ❏ Helmets Are Comfortable!

Following Directions: Follow the Hand Signals

Getting Ready: Teach students the bicycle hand signals found on page 217.
Directions: Play a follow the leader game. Divide students into groups of three or four. Have students in each group line up to play follow the leader. The leader must give hand signals when turning, stopping, and slowing. The leader must also signal obstacles. Make sure everyone has the opportunity to be the leader.

Transportation Music: An Action Song

Need: Transportation Patterns reproducibles (pages 237 and 238), sturdy paper or light cardboard, paper cutter, scissors, craft sticks, tape
Getting Ready: Reproduce the pictures of the 10 vehicles on heavy paper or light cardboard and cut them apart on the dashed lines. Make one set of 10 pictures for each student.
Directions:
1. Have students cut out the vehicles and tape a craft stick handle to the back of each one.
2. Then, teach everyone the words to the last verse of "The Transportation Song," singing to the tune of "The Wheels on the Bus."
    Without machines to move and haul, move and haul, move and haul,
    Without machines to move and haul, there'd be few things for us at all.
3. Next, introduce the sound that each of the 10 vehicles makes.
    semitruck—growls and roars   fire truck—clangs, clangs, clangs
    freighter—honk, honk, honks   ambulance—wooo, wooo, wooos
    train—chug, chug, chugs   jet plane—zoom, zoom, zooms
    car—putt, putt, putts   taxi—beep, beep, beeps
    rocket ship—siss, siss, sisses   subway train—rattles and clacks
4. Explain to students that they should hold up each vehicle as you sing that vehicle's name in the verse. Then, they should make the vehicle's sound three times and then one more time when you pause in the song.
    Leader: *The semitruck, it*—(pause)
    Students: *growls and roars, growls and roars, growls and roars.*
    Leader: *The semitruck, it*—(pause)
    Students: *growls and roars*
    Leader: *hauling loads of freight to stores.*
5. Sing the story as students hold up the correct vehicles and make appropriate sounds. Have everyone join together to sing the last verse.

Drama: Perform "The Transportation Song"

Need: large cardboard boxes, pencils, scissors, crayons, yarn, hole punch
Getting Ready: Help students create vehicle costumes.
1. On a large sheet of cardboard have each student draw and color a large vehicle.
2. Punch two holes in the top of each cardboard vehicle and one hole on each side. Cut two long pieces of yarn. On each side, thread one piece of yarn through the side hole and top hole and tie securely to create armhole loops. The student should slip his arms through the loops and hold each side of the vehicle to steady it.
Directions: Practice "The Transportation Song" with sound effects and costumes. Then, have students perform the song for parents or another class.

Outdoor Adventure: Bike Safety Meet

Getting Ready: Invite students who have bikes, scooters, or tricycles to bring them to school. Before students arrive, set up a simple obstacle course on the blacktop or other smooth play area using orange cones or cardboard boxes painted with bright orange stripes.
Directions: When riders arrive, review hand signals and go over the on-the-road bike safety tips on the Bike Safety Rules reproducible (page 236). When all of the rules have been discussed, students may take turns riding or walking their vehicles through the obstacle course.

Imagination: It's a Trip!

Directions: Invite students to lie back and relax. Instruct them to close their eyes and listen carefully to try to see with their imaginations the sights and sounds on the trips you will describe. To give students time to use their visual memories and imaginations, pause at least 20 seconds after each description.

1. You are riding home on a school bus. It is noisy. It is crowded. It is hot. (pause)
2. You are on a train traveling along in the country. You look out the window and see cows grazing in green grass. You can hear the train whistle and the chug of the engine. (pause)
3. You are riding in the back of a fire truck with three firefighters. You zoom past cars and trucks on your way to a burning building. The siren is loud. The ride is bumpy. (pause)
4. You are on a crowded subway. It is nighttime. You look at the others in your car. (pause)
5. You are an astronaut in a rocket ship. It is ready to blast off. You feel the vibration as the rocket boosters ignite and you hear the roar of the engine. (pause)
6. You are in the back of an ambulance. The loud wailing of the siren hurts your ears but you can't cover them. You need your hands to assist the paramedics. They are helping a man who was in an accident. (pause)
7. You are sitting in the passenger's seat in a huge semi. The driver is listening to country western music and singing. The blacktop road and desert sand stretch as far as you can see into the distance. It is very hot out there, but the cab is cooled by an air conditioner. Icy air is blowing in your face. (pause)
8. You are in your family's car. Look to see who is driving. Imagine where you are going. (pause)
9. You are on a jet going to Hawaii. The steward hands you a little tray of food. Imagine what foods are on the tray. (pause) You are listening to music with earphones. Imagine the music. (pause)
10. You are standing on the deck of a cruise ship. Imagine where it is going. Look out at the blue sea. Imagine the sights and sounds of being where there is no land in sight. (pause)

Critical Thinking: Walking Is Good for You!

Directions: Begin by discussing the type of transportation used by nearly everyone, nearly every day—walking! Explain that you will make some statements about walking. If students think the statement is true, they should give a thumbs-up. Thumbs-down means the statement is false.

1. Walking is an excellent mode of transportation because it is free—it doesn't take gas. *(true)*
2. Walking is an excellent mode of transportation because it is never dangerous. *(false)*
3. Walking is a good mode of transportation because you can get heavy things from one place to another. *(false)*
4. Walking is an excellent mode of transportation because it is good exercise. *(true)*
5. Walking is an excellent mode of transportation because you can get places very quickly. *(false)*
6. Walking should always be done on sidewalks or, if on a road, facing traffic so that you can see oncoming cars. *(true)*
7. When walking during the daytime, you should wear brightly colored clothing. *(true)*
8. When walking at night, you should wear special reflective material on your shoes, cap, or jacket that will reflect the headlights of cars coming towards you. *(true)*
9. When crossing a street, you should cross only at corners or marked crosswalks. *(true)*
10. Before crossing the street, you should stop, look left, look right, look left again, and then cross carefully. *(true)*
11. You should always keep looking for cars while you are crossing a street. *(true)*
12. When crossing a street, you should always run to get to the other side quickly. *(false)*

Directions for Reproducible Activity Pages

Visual Memory: Stop and Go—Page 231

Need: Stop and Go reproducible (page 231); red, yellow, and green construction paper; scissors; tape; craft sticks; pencils; crayons; glue sticks

Getting Ready: Cut out three large circles, one each from the red, yellow, and green construction paper. Tape a craft stick handle to the back of each one. Review the meanings of traffic light colors with students: red means stop; yellow means slow down and then stop; green means go. To play Stop and Go, have students stand and march in place. Hold up the construction paper signals to communicate the marchers' speed and when they should stop and go.

Directions: Pass out page 231. Together, read aloud the traffic direction words in the circles on the worksheet. Then, instruct students to color the three circles the correct colors. Have students cut out the circles on the dashed lines and glue them in the correct order on the traffic light.

Critical Thinking: What's Wrong?—Page 232

Need: What's Wrong? reproducible (page 232), pencils, crayons

Directions: Pass out page 232. Begin by explaining that there are eight mistakes in the picture. Students should find each mistake and circle it. Then, they may color the picture any colors they choose.

Follow-Up: After students have completed the worksheets, meet in a large group and take turns sharing ideas about how the mistakes shown in the picture could be corrected.

Critical Thinking: Which One?—Page 233

Need: Which One? reproducible (page 233), crayons

Directions: Pass out page 233. Read each direction aloud as students work independently. Be sure to allow plenty of time for students to complete each question before reading the next direction.

Follow-Up: After students have completed the worksheets, meet in large group to discuss each answer.

Following Directions: Bicycle Hand Signals—Page 234

Need: Bicycle Hand Signals reproducible (page 234), crayons

Getting Ready: Draw the bicycle hand signals below on the board and label them.

Directions: Begin by teaching students the bicycle hand signals. Practice giving a command while students make the appropriate hand signal.

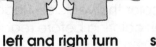

left and right turn   **stopping or slowing**   **railroad crossing ahead**   **pothole or debris on left and right**

Next, pass out page 234 and read the following directions aloud. Be sure to allow plenty of time for students to complete each question independently before reading the next direction.

1. A biker signals to bikers riding behind him that there is a pothole on the left or right. Circle these signals with purple.
2. A biker signals that she is going to turn left or right. Circle these signals with yellow.
3. A biker signals that he is going to slow down and stop. Circle this signal with red.
4. A biker signals that there is a railroad crossing ahead. Circle this signal with blue.

Directions for Reproducible Activity Pages, CONTINUED

Connecting with Family: Six Steps for Bike Checks—page 235

Need: Six Bike Safety Checks reproducible (page 235), crayons

Directions: Pass out page 235. Read aloud the six steps for bike checks, stopping to discuss each one. Have students color the area on each bike to indicate where the bike should be checked. Encourage students to take home their lists and, with an adult, mark each box after the appropriate bike part on their own bikes has been checked.

Follow-Up: Back in class, discuss things students found that needed repair on their bikes and how they fixed them.

Following Directions: Bike Safety Rules—Page 236

Need: Bike Safety Rules reproducible (page 236), crayons, pencils

Directions: Pass out page 236. One at a time, read aloud each bike safety rule and then give the student direction (below). After a discussion of each safety rule, have students select one of the rules to illustrate on the backs of their papers.

Bike Safety Rules:

1. When it comes to the rules of the road, a bike is a like a car. Obey all traffic signs and signals. Circle the one way sign with blue.
2. Bikes, like cars, must stop at stop signs and red lights. Circle the stop sign with red.
3. Bikers must learn to see and be seen in traffic. Always wear a helmet. Circle the helmet with the same color as your eyes.
4. Bikers must stop and look for traffic when entering the road—especially from driveways, alleys, and curbs. Circle the do not enter sign with red.
5. Bikes must travel with the flow of traffic—ride on the right, the same direction as a car. Draw a green box around the traffic flow sign.
6. Bikers should avoid riding at night and avoid dark conditions, narrow roads, and roads with cars traveling faster than 35 mph. Circle the speed limit sign with purple.
7. If a bike must be ridden at night, the biker should use reflectors, lights, and retroreflective clothing. Circle the reflectors with red.
8. Bikers should always be predictable. They should ride in a straight line. They should look behind them before changing lanes or turning, use a hand signal, and then proceed carefully. Circle the keep right sign with orange.
9. Bikers should walk their bicycles across busy intersections. Circle the no bikes sign with red.
10. Bikers must watch out for dangerous things in the street: wet leaves, puddles, ice, loose gravel, rocks, broken glass, and cracks in the road. Color the detour sign orange.

Following Directions: Transportation Vehicles—Pages 237 and 238

Need: Transportation Patterns reproducibles (pages 237 and 238), crayons, scissors, glue sticks, large sheets of paper

Directions: Tell students to listen carefully to your directions to color the vehicles. Read each direction aloud. Be sure to allow time for students to complete their coloring before reading the next direction.

1. Color the semitruck blue.
2. Color the jet black.
3. Color the fire truck with your red crayon.
4. Color the minivan with your pink crayon.
5. Color the train engine brown.
6. Color the taxi yellow.
7. Color the ambulance with your green crayon.
8. Color the rocket with your purple crayon.
9. Color the freighter orange.
10. Color the subway train black.

Follow-Up: Pass out the large sheets of paper. Have students cut out and arrange their vehicles to create vehicle collages. After gluing the vehicles in place, students may add details such as roads, buildings, or other background scenery.

The Transportation Song

The teacher said, "Kids, sing along, Sing along, sing along." The teacher said, "Kids, sing along, Sing the transportation song."

The semitruck, it growls and roars,
Growls and roars, growls and roars.

The semitruck, it growls and roars,
Hauling loads of freight to stores.

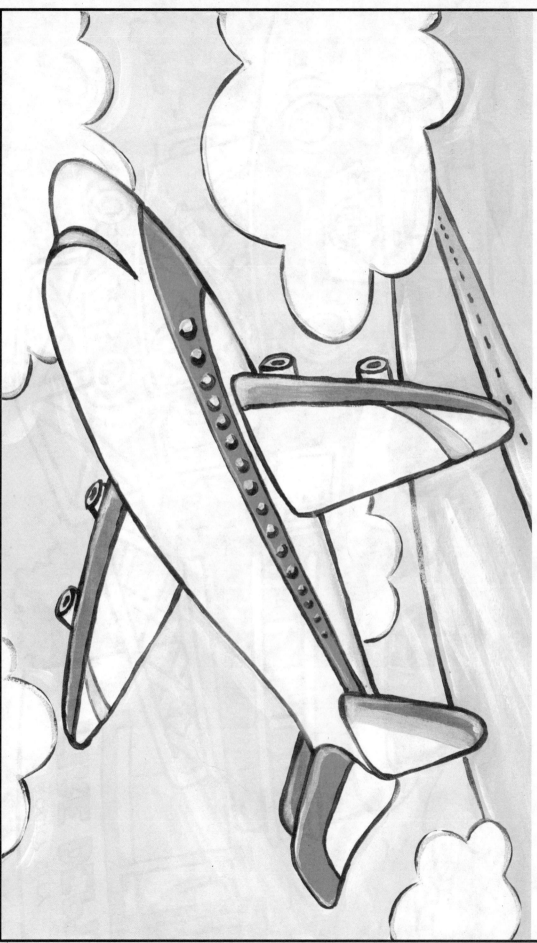

Jet planes speed us through the air,
Through the air, through the air.

Jet planes speed us through the air

Jet planes speed us through the air
And fly us all from here to there.

221

The Brainy Bunch Kids—Learning the Basics

The fire truck wails, "Out of the way,
Out of the way, out of the way."

The fire truck wails, "Out of the way
For there's a fire somewhere today."

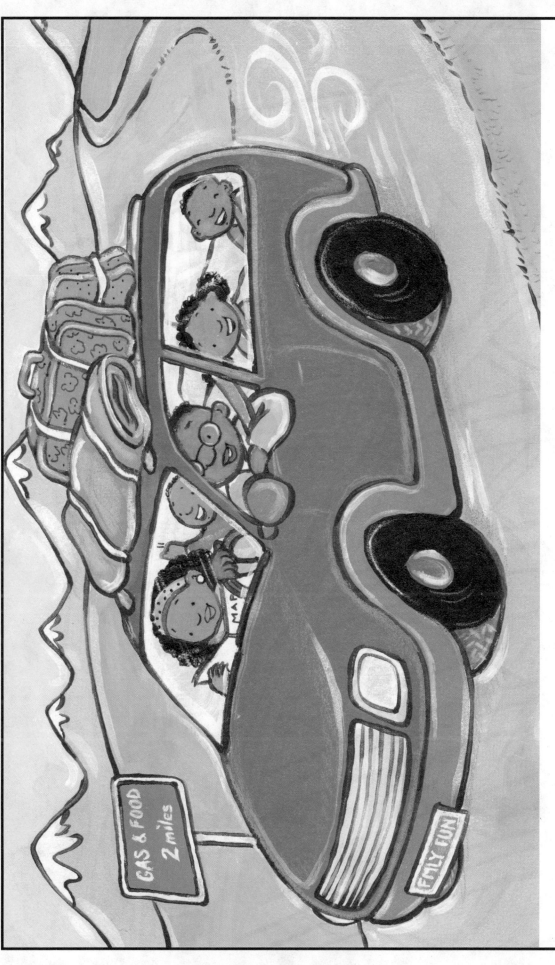

Our motor cars drive to and fro,
To and fro, to and fro.

Our motor cars drive to and fro,
Wherever the family needs to go.

Strings of cars on railroad trains,
Railroad trains, railroad trains,

Strings of cars on railroad trains
Are hauling cattle, coal, and grain.

The taxi hack asks, "Where to, Mac? Where to, Mac? Where to, Mac?"

The taxi hack asks, "Where to, Mac? I will drive you there and back."

225

The ambulance is small and quick,
Small and quick, small and quick.

The ambulance is small and quick
To save your life when you are sick.

Rocket ships have tails of fire,
Tails of fire, tails of fire.

Rocket ships have tails of fire
To lift space shuttles higher and higher.

The Brainy Bunch Kids—Learning the Basics

Ocean freighters sail so slow,
Sail so slow, sail so slow.

Ocean freighters sail so slow
Through ocean waves when
storm winds blow.

KE-804011 © Key Education

The subway train moves
underground,
Underground, underground.

The subway train moves
underground
For workers from all sides of town.

The Brainy Bunch Kids—Learning the Basics

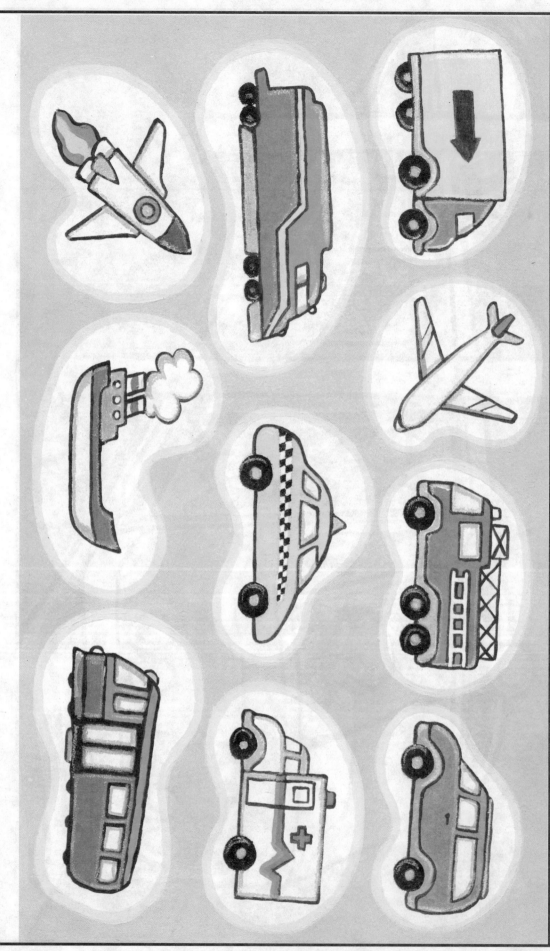

Without machines to move and haul,
Move and haul, move and haul,

Without machines to move and haul,
There'd be few things for us at all.

KE-804011 © Key Education

Name _____   **Date** _____

Stop and Go

Directions: Read the words and color each circle the correct color. Cut out and glue each circle on the correct light.

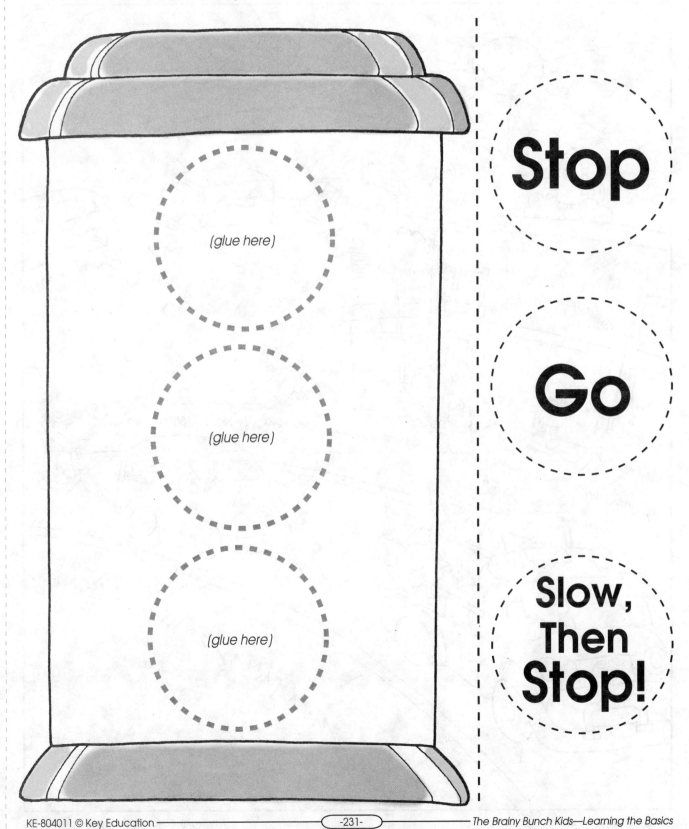

Name _____   **Date** _____

What's Wrong?

Directions: Find eight things wrong in the picture. Circle them. Then, color the picture.

Name _____   **Date** _____

Which One?

Directions: Listen carefully and follow directions.

1. You must travel 3,000 miles to see your grandmother. Which one would get you there the quickest? Circle it in red.

2. Scientists want to go to Mars. Which one would they use? Circle it with your blue crayon.

    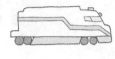

3. A man needs to be rushed to a hospital. Which would get him there quickest? Circle it with purple.

4. Heavy boxes must be moved across the sea. Which would be used? Draw a ring around it with yellow.

5. There is a fire. Which vehicle would rush to the fire first? Draw a red box around it.

6. Your dad wants to drive to work. Which would he drive? Draw a green ring around it.

7. Heavy cars must be moved across the country. What might carry them best? Draw an orange box around it.

     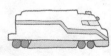

8. Strawberries must be moved from California to Nevada. What might carry them best? Circle it with pink.

Name _____   **Date** _____

(See directions on page 217.)

Bicycle Hand Signals

Directions: Listen carefully and follow directions.

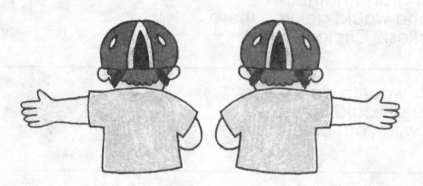

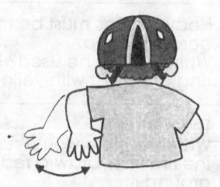

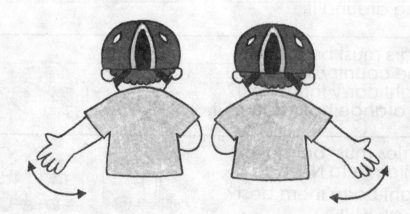

Name _____ **Date** _____

Six Bike Safety Checks

1. Is your bike the proper size? A bike that is too big or too small is difficult to control. When standing on the ground, there should be a 1" to 3" (2.54 cm to 7.62 cm) gap between the rider and the top bar.

2. Is your bike seat adjusted to the proper height? When you are sitting on the seat with a foot on the pedal, your leg should be slightly bent. This will help avoid knee strain.

3. Are there reflectors on the front and rear of your bike? The rear reflector should be red and at least 3" (7.62 cm) wide. Make sure the reflector is pointed straight back to reflect the headlights of cars coming from behind the bike.

4. Is your bike's chain clean and lubricated? If it is not, ask an adult to help you clean and lubricate the chain or take your bike to a local bike shop to be checked.

5. Do your bike's brakes apply even pressure? The brakes should make the bike's back wheel skid on dry pavement, but not stick.

6. Are your bike's tires properly inflated?

Name _____   **Date** _____

(See directions on page 218.)

Bike Safety Rules

Directions: Listen carefully to the bike safety rules and follow the directions.

1. When it comes to the rules of the road, a bike is a like a car. Obey all traffic signs and signals.

2. Bikes, like cars, must stop at stop signs and red lights.

3. Bikers must learn to see and be seen in traffic. Always wear a helmet.

4. Bikers must stop and look for traffic when entering the road—especially from driveways, alleys, and curbs.

5. Bikes must travel with the flow of traffic—ride on the right, the same direction as a car.

6. Bikers should avoid riding at night and avoid dark conditions, narrow roads, and roads with cars traveling faster than 35 mph.

7. If a bike must be ridden at night, the biker should use reflectors, lights, and retroreflective clothing.

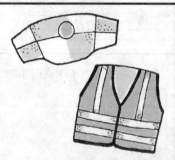

8. Bikers should always be predictable. They should ride in a straight line. They should look behind them before changing lanes or turning, use a hand signal, and then proceed carefully.

9. Bikers should walk their bicycles across busy intersections.

10. Bikers must watch out for dangerous things in the street: wet leaves, puddles, ice, loose gravel, rocks, broken glass, and cracks in the road.

Name _____   **Date** _____

(See directions on pages 215 and 218.)

Transportation Patterns

Directions: Listen carefully and follow directions.

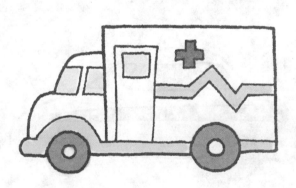
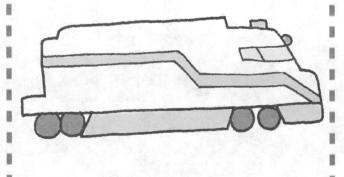

Name _____ **Date** _____

(See directions on pages 215 and 218.)

Transportation Patterns

Directions: Listen carefully and follow directions.

Chapter 10—The Farm
(Teacher's Guide)

Learning Center: Setting the Stage for the Pullout Story "Uncle Eual's Huge Blue Mule"

Need: outdoor garden plot; vegetable/flower seeds and plants; gardening tools: hoes, rakes, shovels, hand trowels, watering containers; record keeping equipment: measuring tapes or string, magnifying glasses, pencils, graph paper, garden journal notebooks

Directions: For an excellent learning center to celebrate farms, provide a small garden plot where students can plant seeds and seedlings. This hands-on learning center—a place for investigating and experimenting—will empower children in a wholesome way. As the plants grow, so will students' interest in plants, ecosystems, and the world.

Gardening Tips:
1. Locate and, with the help of students, prepare a small outdoor garden plot.
2. Discuss and make a list of the vegetables and flowers students would like to grow.
3. Reproduce the list and send it home so that parents may contribute seeds and seedlings or gardening tools.
4. Make the gardening tools and record keeping equipment easily accessible.
5. In the beginning, motivate everyone by sprouting fast-growing seeds such as beans or lentils.
6. Plant sensory and unusual plants such as spearmint and nasturtiums, which have edible flowers and leaves. Also, grow vegetables that students may have never tasted: turnips, rutabagas, chives, radishes, etc.
7. Provide opportunities for students to take risks, explore, make choices, and cooperate.
8. Keep investigations and projects ongoing and overlap them.
9. Observe and discuss the changes that take place in the garden.
10. Celebrate all successful attempts to grow plants and learn from unsuccessful attempts.
11. Harvest vegetables, wash them thoroughly, and cut them into tiny chunks so that everyone may have a taste.

Caution: Before completing any food activity, ask families' permission and inquire about students' food allergies and religious or other food preferences.

Outdoor Adventure: How High?

Need: outdoor garden plot or planting pots, seeds, craft sticks, pen

Directions: Have a growing contest. Allow each child to plant his choice of three seeds of his choosing. (Parents may help students decide what kinds of seed to plant.) Clearly mark each growing area with the student's name written on a craft stick. Students should water, weed around, and stake their plants as needed. Each Friday, measure the plants and record the growth on a class chart. At the end of 30 days, discuss which kinds of plants grew the most.

Field Trip Ideas: Farm Friendly

During your study on produce and livestock, arrange for students to visit a farm or ranch. If this is not possible, visit one of the following places to celebrate growing things.
- ❑ fair with 4-H animals and produce
- ❑ plant nursery
- ❑ neighborhood garden, orchard, or vineyard
- ❑ local farmers' market

Companion Book: *Busy in the Garden*

"Zucchini meeny miney moe. Plant a seed and watch it grow."

Need: *Busy in the Garden* by George Shannon (Greenwillow Books)

Directions: Share the 24 delightful rhyming verses and riddles in the companion book. Allow those who so wish to illustrate some of the verses.

Other Good Books to Share:
- ❑ *Eddie's Garden and How to Make Things Grow* by Sarah Garland (Frances Lincoln Children's Books)
- ❑ *Salad People and More Real Recipes: A New Cookbook for Preschoolers & Up* by Mollie Katzen (Tricycle Press)

Presenting the Pullout Story: "Uncle Eual's Huge Blue Mule"

Need: "Uncle Eual's Huge Blue Mule" story (page 245–256)

Directions: Read the story to the class one page at a time without sharing the illustrations. Instead, pause in each verse just before naming the animal or animals each Brainy found. Invite students to guess what animal was in each location. Then, show the class the illustration to see if they were correct as you reread the lines.

Music: Sing "Uncle Eual Had a Farm"

Directions: Sing a new song to the tune of "Old MacDonald Had a Farm." Sing a verse about each of the 10 types of animals in the story: a cat and kittens (meow), hens (cluck), piglets (oink) a dog (arf), ducks (quack), a snake (hiss), sheep (baa), mice (squeak), a goat (bleat), and a huge blue mule (bray).

Uncle Eual had a farm, E-I-E-I-O.
And on his farm he had some kittens, E-I-E-I-O
With a "meow, meow" here and a "meow, meow" there,
Here a "meow," there a "meow,"
Everywhere a "meow, meow."
Uncle Eual had a farm, E-I-E-I-O.

Bulletin Board: On the Farm Mural

Need: bulletin board, roll of blue paper, black construction paper, 4" to 6" (10 cm to 15 cm) letter patterns, scissors, crayons, markers, paints, colored chalk, stapler or tape

Getting Ready: Cover a bulletin board or wall with blue paper. Trace letter patterns on black paper and cut them out to make the title. Center the title at the top of the board. Draw and color a large red barn in the center of the board.

Directions: Have students use paints, crayons, markers, or colored chalk to draw farm animals—especially those featured in the story—on the mural. They may also include plants, such as crops or trees, and other background details.

Drama: A Choral Reading

Directions: Reread the story. Then, help students memorize the last two lines of the first 10 verses.
"But they/she/he could not locate Jewel,
Uncle Eual's huge blue mule."

Read the story again; this time as you reach the last two lines in each verse, point to the class. They should respond in unison with the last two lines. Remind students that they will have to pay close attention to the verse to know if they should say *they, she,* or *he.*

Listening Skills: Sounds on the Farm

Directions: Make a variety of farm-animal sounds and have students take turns identifying the animal that makes each sound. When students know how to play the game, let them take turns making animal sounds for others to guess. You may expand the game to include any animal—not just farm animals. The child who guesses correctly makes the next sound.

Examples:

1. geese—cackle, hiss, honk	6. donkey/mule—bray	11. sheep/lamb—bleat, baa
2. goat—bleat	7. horse—neigh, whinny	12. pig—grunt, squeal
3. cat—meow, mew, purr	8. hen—peep, cackle, cluck	13. snake—hiss
4. cow—moo	9. mice—squeak	14. rooster—crow
5. turkey—gobble	10. dog—bark, woof, arf	15. duck—quack

Story Recall: Did They See It?

Directions: Reread the story, "Uncle Eual's Huge Blue Mule." Then, explain that you will name things that might or might not be found on farms. If the object was found on the farm in the story, students should shade their eyes with one of their hands to indicate they could see it. If not, students should close their eyes and cover them with one of their hands.

1. barn *(see)*	7. hen pens *(see)*	13. mice *(see)*	19. mud hole *(see)*
2. lion *(not see)*	8. snake *(see)*	14. hippopotamus *(not see)*	20. mule *(see)*
3. dog *(see)*	9. log by the lake *(see)*	15. swimming hole *(see)*	21. Uncle Eual *(see)*
4. ducks *(see)*	10. sheep *(see)*	16. hamster *(not see)*	22. Aunt Eual *(not see)*
5. hens *(see)*	11. elephant *(not see)*	17. alligator *(not see)*	23. goat *(see)*
6. kittens *(see)*	12. rusty truck *(see)*	18. piglets *(see)*	24. haystack *(see)*

Listening Skills: The Same Last Sound

Directions: Discuss the fact that some words have the same ending sound or sounds. Give some examples such as *cat* and *bat*, *boy* and *toy*, and *see* and *me*. Next, tell students to listen carefully as you name two animals. If the animals' names end with the same sound, students should give a thumbs-up. Thumbs-down means the animals' names do not end with the same sound.

1. cat, rat	9. eagle, beagle	17. lamb, sheep	24. hippopotamus, rhinoceros
2. snake, snail	10. bee, flea	18. mouse, horse	25. goat, mule
3. frog, dog	11. hog, frog	19. gnat, rat	26. flea, tick
4. buffalo, mosquito	12. zebra, fish	20. worm, bird	27. octopus, platypus
5. crow, dodo	13. monkey, donkey	21. armadillo, flamingo	28. dingo, rhino
6. cobra, boa	14. ant, elephant	22. llama, zebra	29. badger, tiger
7. tiger, lion	15. goat, giraffe	23. iguana, gorilla	30. grasshopper, roadrunner
8. cobra, chimpanzee	16. pony, horse		

Game: Name a Rhymer

Need: Short and Long Vowel Animal Picture Cards reproducible (page 263), white sturdy paper, paper cutter, rubber band

Getting Ready: On white sturdy paper, reproduce page 263 for each student. Use a paper cutter to cut apart each set of animal picture cards and secure it with a rubber band.

Directions: Begin by holding up each of the cards and naming the animal: cat, hen, pig, dog, duck, snake, sheep, mice, goat, and mule. Then, hold up one card at a time and have students take turns saying a word that rhymes with the animal's name. (If *duck* might prove a problem in your class, take that picture card out.) After students know how to play the game, pair them and have them challenge their partners to name rhyming words for each of the long and short vowel animal names.

Imagination: Visit Uncle Eual's Farm

Directions: Invite students to lie back and relax. Instruct them to close their eyes and listen carefully to try to see with their imaginations what you will describe. To give students time to use their visual memories and imaginations, pause 20 to 30 seconds after each description.

1. It's early morning in the summertime. You are sleeping on Uncle Eual's back porch. The sun is coming up and you can hear a rooster crowing—cock-a-doodle-doo! (pause)
2. You roll out of bed and go into the kitchen. Uncle Eual is frying bacon in a big iron skillet. Can you smell the bacon? Can you hear it sizzle? (pause)
3. You sit down at a long wood table. Uncle Eual hands you a plate stacked high with pancakes. You slather butter on top. As the butter melts, you pour on thick maple syrup. Can you see the stack of pancakes? (pause)
4. You use a big fork to cut a bite of pancakes and stuff it into your mouth. You chew slowly and then swallow. Take another bite. Imagine how good the pancakes taste. (pause)
5. Uncle Eual pours a glass of your favorite juice. You drink it all. How do you feel? (pause)
6. Uncle Eual sits down at the table and tells you that you will both be riding horses all day. You will work with cattle and fix barbwire fences. How does that sound to you? (pause)
7. Now, it is much later. The sun is slipping out of the sky. You've been on horseback all day. You are hot, tired, and hungry. Back at the farmhouse, you sink into a bathtub of warm, soapy water. You just rest there, thinking about the hard work you and Uncle Eual did today. (pause)
8. You get out of the tub, dry off, slip on pajamas, and go into the kitchen for supper. (pause)
9. After you finish eating meat-and-potato stew, you go back onto the porch and crawl into bed. You snuggle down under the quilt and listen for the night sounds. What do you hear? (pause)
10. You look up and see the stars. Between you and the stars, fireflies flicker. (pause)
11. You fall asleep. What do you dream about? (pause)

Visual Memory: How Big? So-o-o-o Big!

Directions: Gather students on the floor around you. Tell them you will name different animals, and, as they listen, they should think about each animal's size. Then, they should show the animal's size by using a finger and thumb (tiny), holding their hands apart (medium), or extending their arms (huge). Allow time for the discussion of any differing answers.

1. rabbit (medium)
2. frog (tiny)
3. bee (tiny)
4. mule (huge)
5. cat (medium)
6. kitten (medium)
7. duck (medium)
8. giraffe (huge)
9. snake (medium)
10. dog (medium)
11. kangaroo (huge)
12. piglet (medium)
13. snail (tiny)
14. spider (tiny)
15. horse (huge)
16. bat (tiny)
17. tick (tiny)
18. lamb (medium)
19. elephant (huge)
20. rhinoceros (huge)
21. ladybug (tiny)
22. hen (medium)
23. whale (huge)
24. goat (medium)
25. mouse (tiny)
26. gnat (tiny)
27. hippopotamus (huge)
28. lion (huge)
29. alligator (huge)
30. dragonfly (tiny)
31. llama (huge)
32. whale (huge)
33. dodo (medium)
34. dinosaur (medium or huge)
35. butterfly (tiny)
36. eel (medium)
37. goldfish (tiny)
38. gorilla (huge)
39. goose (medium)
40. zebra (huge)

Game: About That Size

Directions: Gather students on the floor around you. As you name animals (see the list above), invite students to name another animal that is approximately the same size—tiny, medium, or huge. Then, play again. This time ask students to name an animal that can be the same color as each animal on the list.

Follow-Up: Name three of the animals listed above. Have students take turns naming the three animals again in order of size, from smallest to largest. For example, if you say, "duck, goat, tick," a student should respond, "tick, duck, goat."

Snack: How Does Your Garden Grow?

Need: vegetable sticks and fruit chunks or bread and nut butter

Directions: In large group, name each food listed below. Have students use hand motions to indicate if the food grows in a garden, field, or orchard or if it is manufactured with a variety of ingredients. If the food grows in a garden, field, or orchard, students should wiggle entwined hands and arms to pantomime a plant growing up from the ground. If the food is a combination of many ingredients, students should pantomime combining the ingredients in a big bowl and stirring them.

1. potato (garden)
2. macaroni and cheese (combination)
3. bread (combination)
4. green beans (garden)
5. turnip (garden)
6. cantaloupe (garden)
7. orange (orchard)
8. pizza (combination)
9. corn (garden or field)
10. pie (combination)
11. doughnut (combination)
12. lettuce (garden)
13. sweet potato (garden)
14. cake (combination)
15. celery (garden)
16. muffin (combination)
17. carrot (garden)
18. apple (orchard)
19. hamburger and bun (combination)
20. peach cobbler (combination)
21. peas (garden)
22. wheat (field)
23. grapes (garden)
24. vegetable soup (combination)
25. deviled egg (combination)
26. ice cream (combination)
27. watermelon (garden)
28. hot dog and bun (combination)
29. onion (garden)
30. peanuts (field)
31. pineapple punch (combination)

Follow-Up: Serve a snack of vegetable sticks and fruit chunks or nut-butter sandwiches.

Caution: Before completing any food activity, ask families' permission and inquire about students' food allergies and religious or other food preferences.

Critical Thinking: How Does It Move?

Getting Ready: Teach students the following movements.

swim—move arms as if swimming **fly**—flap arms like wings

hop—move upper body up and down **run**—while seated, move legs as if running

Directions: Name an animal from the list below. One at a time, ask students if the animal can swim, fly, hop, or run, pausing after naming each movement. If the animal can move in the specified way, students respond with their own matching movements. If the animal does not move in the specified way, students should remain still.

1. frog (swim, hop)
2. fish (swim)
3. rabbit (swim, hop, run)
4. cat (swim, run)
5. duck (swim, fly, run)
6. snake (swim)
7. kangaroo (swim, hop)
8. mule (swim, run)
9. dog (swim, run)
10. hen (fly, run)

Critical Thinking: Plant or Animal?

Directions: One at a time, name the foods listed below. Have students show with the following movements whether each food comes from an animal or plant. If the food comes from an animal, students should bend over with hanging arms like an animal with four legs. If the food comes from a plant, students should wiggle entwined hands and arms to pantomime growing up from the ground.

1. hamburger (animal)
2. carrot (plant)
3. pepperoni (animal)
4. bread (plant)
5. bologna (animal)
6. hot dog (animal)
7. grapes (plant)
8. spinach (plant)
9. pork chop (animal)
10. fish stick (animal)
11. broccoli (plant)
12. orange (plant)
13. raisins (plant)
14. steak (animal)
15. potato (plant)
16. lettuce salad (plant)
17. ham (animal)
18. roast (animal)
19. mushroom (plant)
20. fruit salad (plant)
21. apple juice (plant)
22. fig jam (plant)
23. pasta (plant)
24. french fries (plant)
25. drumstick (animal)

Directions for Reproducible Activity Pages

Visual Memory: Illustrate Uncle Eual's Huge Blue Mule—Pages 257 and 258

Need: Uncle Eual's Huge Blue Mule booklet reproducibles (pages 257 and 258), white sturdy paper, paper cutter, crayons, stapler

Getting Ready: On white sturdy paper, reproduce pages 257 and 258 for each student. Use a paper cutter to cut apart each set of 12 minipages. Make sure the pages are in order and staple each set in the upper left-hand corner to create a booklet.

Directions: Pass out the booklets and reread the story aloud as students follow along. Allow time for students to illustrate and color each page.

Story Recall: Uncle Eual's Farm—Page 259

Need: Uncle Eual's Farm reproducible (page 259), pencils, crayons

Directions: Pass out page 259. After reading the story, invite students to draw the animals in the appropriate places to finish the picture. You may make copies of the story for students to use for reference.

Follow-Up: When students have completed their pictures, meet in large group. Use the worksheets to reinforce position words. Ask the following questions.

1. What animals were in the hayloft?
   (a cat with kittens)
2. What animals were by the truck?
   (six quacking ducks)
3. What animal was in the swimming hole?
   (Jewel, the huge blue mule)
4. What animal was down by the lake?
   (a fat black snake)

5. What animal was beneath the tree?
   (a dog with fleas)
6. What animals were inside the corncrib?
   (baby mice)
7. What animals were upon the hillside?
   (grazing sheep)
8. What animals were on their nests?
   (laying hens)

Critical Thinking: Farm or Zoo?—Page 260

Need: Farm or Zoo? reproducible (page 260), crayons

Directions: Pass out page 260 and read the directions aloud to students. Allow them to complete the page independently.

Following Directions: Hidden Creatures—Page 261

Need: Hidden Creatures reproducible (page 261), crayons

Directions: Pass out page 261. Explain to students that they need to listen carefully to find the hidden pictures. Allow plenty of time for students to complete each direction before reading the next. After following the six directions, encourage students to color the page any colors they choose.

1. Circle one skunk with black.
2. Circle two bees with yellow.
3. Circle five beehives with purple.

4. Circle two mules with blue.
5. Circle four dinosaurs with orange.
6. Circle five chicks with green.

Fine Motor: I Can Print Animal Words—Page 262

Need: I Can Print Animal Words reproducible (page 262), pencils, crayons

Directions: Pass out page 262 and read aloud the directions. Have students trace each animal word. Then, invite them to read the words to a friend.

Game: Vowel Rummy—Pages 263 and 264

Need: Short and Long Vowel Animal Picture Cards reproducible (page 263) and Short and Long Vowel Animal Word Cards reproducible (page 264), sturdy paper, paper cutter, rubber bands

Getting Ready: On sturdy paper, reproduce two copies each of pages 263 and 264 for each group of two to three students.

How to Play:

1. Divide students into groups of two or three. Shuffle and deal each player eight cards. Place the remaining cards facedown in a stack.
2. Players take turns drawing and discarding cards in an attempt to make sets of four matching cards—two word cards and two picture cards. The first player to get two sets calls "Rummy!" and wins the game.

UNCLE EUAL'S HUGE BLUE MULE

Chapter 10—
The Farm

JEWEL

BOSSY

The Brainies met upon the farm
And hurried down toward the barn;

But they could not locate Jewel,
Uncle Eual's huge blue mule.

In the hayloft, partly hidden,
Jada found a cat with kittens;
But she could not locate Jewel,
Uncle Eual's huge blue mule.

On their nests, inside their pens,
Eli spied some laying hens;

But he could not locate Jewel,
Uncle Eual's huge blue mule.

The Brainy Bunch Kids—Learning the Basics

In a mud hole, Yuuto found
Several piglets, fat and round;
But he could not locate Jewel,
Uncle Eual's huge blue mule.

They saw a dog beneath a tree   But they could not locate Jewel,
In the shadows, scratching fleas;   Uncle Eual's huge blue mule.

By an old-time, rusting truck,
Zoe scared six quacking ducks;

But she could not locate Jewel,
Uncle Eual's huge blue mule.

Beneath a log, down by the lake,
Eli chased a fat black snake;

But he could not locate Jewel,
Uncle Eual's huge blue mule.

251

Upon a hillside, green and steep,
Zoe petted grazing sheep;

But she could not locate Jewel,
Uncle Eual's huge blue mule.

Inside a corncrib, Jada peeked
At baby mice all blind and weak;

But she could not locate Jewel,
Uncle Eual's huge blue mule.

Yuuto saw a billy goat
Munching on some poison oak;

But he could not locate Jewel,
Uncle Eual's huge blue mule.

Up to Eual, they trudged back
To where he pitched hay
on a stack.

"Won't you help us, Uncle Eual?
We want to ride your huge
blue mule."

The Brainy Bunch Kids—Learning the Basics

Eual took them for a stroll
Down beside the swimming hole.

In the middle, there was Jewel,
Uncle Eual's huge blue mule.

KE-804011 © Key Education

ABC·123·▲·■ ABC·123·▲·● ABC·123·▲·■ ABC·123·▲·● ABC·123·▲·■ ABC·123·▲·● ABC·123·▲·■ ABC·123·▲·● ABC·123·▲·■ ABC·123·▲·● ABC·123·▲·■ ABC·123·▲·● ABC123·▲·■ ABC·123·▲·● ABC·123·▲·■ ABC·123·▲·● ABC·123·▲·■ ABC·123·▲·●

(See directions on page 244.)

Uncle Eual's Huge Blue Mule

The Brainies met upon the farm
And hurried down toward the barn;
But they could not locate Jewel,
Uncle Eual's huge blue mule.

-1-

In the hayloft, partly hidden,
Jada found a cat with kittens;
But she could not locate Jewel,
Uncle Eual's huge blue mule.

-2-

On their nests, inside their pens,
Eli spied some laying hens;
But he could not locate Jewel,
Uncle Eual's huge blue mule.

-3-

In a mud hole, Yuuto found
Several piglets, fat and round;
But he could not locate Jewel,
Uncle Eual's huge blue mule.

-4-

They saw a dog beneath a tree
In the shadows, scratching fleas;
But they could not locate Jewel,
Uncle Eual's huge blue mule.

-5-

By an old-time, rusting truck,
Zoe scared six quacking ducks;
But she could not locate Jewel,
Uncle Eual's huge blue mule.

-6-

(See directions on page 244.)

Beneath a log, down by the lake,
Eli chased a fat black snake;
But he could not locate Jewel,
Uncle Eual's huge blue mule.

-7-

Upon a hillside, green and steep,
Zoe petted grazing sheep.
But she could not locate Jewel,
Uncle Eual's huge blue mule.

-8-

Insided a corncrib, Jada peeked
At baby mice all blind and weak;
But she could not locate Jewel,
Uncle Eual's huge blue mule.

-9-

Yuuto saw a billy goat
Munching on some poison oak;
But he could not locate Jewel,
Uncle Eual's huge blue mule.

-10-

Up to Eual, they trudged back
To where he pitched hay on a stack.
"Won't you help us, Uncle Eaul?
We want to ride your huge blue mule."

-11-

Eual took them for a stroll
Down beside the swimming hole.
In the middle, there was Jewel,
Uncle Eual's huge blue mule.

-12-

Name

Date

Uncle Eual's Farm

Directions: Listen to the story. Draw the animals in the correct places.

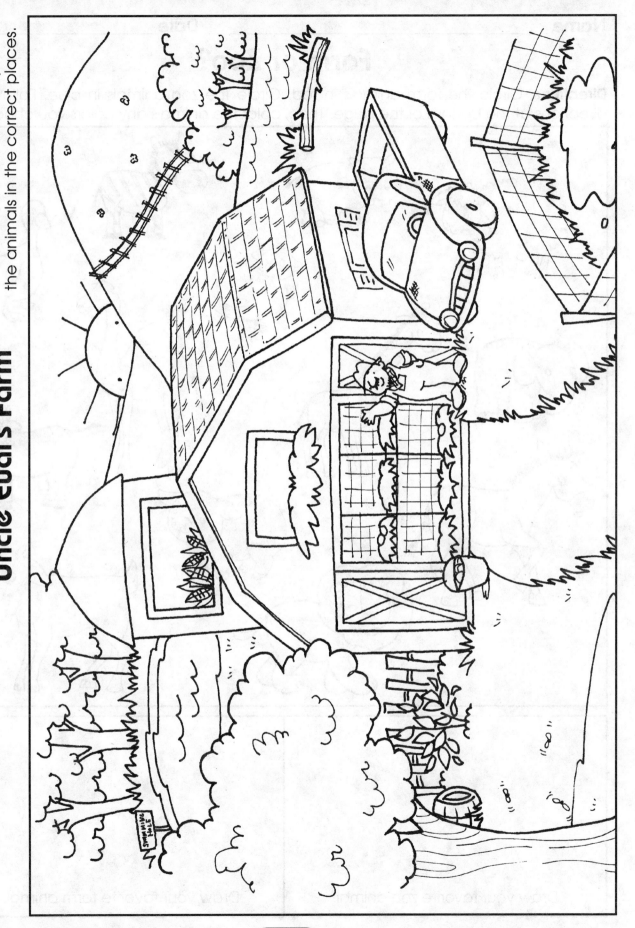

Name _____   **Date** _____

Farm or Zoo?

Directions: Circle the farm animals in red. Circle the zoo animals in blue. Follow the directions at the bottom of the page. Then, color the animals any colors you choose.

Draw your favorite zoo animal.

Draw your favorite farm animal.

Name _____ **Date** _____

(See directions on page 244.)

Hidden Creatures

Directions: Listen carefully and follow directions.

Name _____ **Date** _____

I Can Print Animal Words

Directions: Use a pencil to trace each animal word. Then, read the words to a friend.

cat cat

pig pig

hen hen

dog dog

duck duck

snake

sheep

goat goat

mice mice

mule mule

(See directions on pages 138, 241, and 244.)

Short and Long Vowel Animal Picture Cards

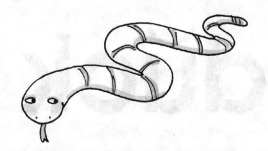

(See directions on page 244.)

Short and Long Vowel Animal Word Cards

căt

hĕn

pĭg

dŏg

dŭck

snāke

shēep

mīce

gōat

mūle

Chapter 11—Water
(Teacher's Guide)

Learning Center: Setting the Stage for the Pullout Story: "The Science Fair"

Need: table and shelves for supplies

Directions: A learning center to celebrate science might include several of the following:

- ❑ jars of bubble mixture and bubble wands
- ❑ eight water glasses forming an instrument that spans an octave
- ❑ a mirror secured in water and a flashlight for projecting a rainbow on a piece of paper
- ❑ a tub of water with objects to float and sink

Good Books to Share:

- ❑ *All the Colors of the Rainbow* by Allan Fowler (Children's Press)
- ❑ *Let's Try It Out in the Water: Hands-On Early-Learning Science Activities* by Seymour Simon and Nicole Fauteux (Simon & Schuster Books for Young Readers)
- ❑ *The Incredible Water Show* by Debra Frasier (Harcourt)
- ❑ *Pop! A Book about Bubbles* by Kimberly Brubaker Bradley (HarperCollins)
- ❑ *This Is the Rain* by Lola M. Schaefer (Greenwillow Books)
- ❑ *Water: Up, Down, and All Around* by Natalie M. Rosinsky (Picture Window Books)

Field Trip Ideas: Take the Drive and Dive

Any of the following excursions will celebrate water science.

- ❑ Visit a brook, pond, lake, sea, etc.
- ❑ Visit an aquarium or pond-supply store.
- ❑ Visit a science museum.

Presenting the Pullout Story: "The Science Fair"

Need: "The Science Fair" story (pages 271–282); Brainy Bunch Puppet Patterns reproducibles (pages 315–318); flannel board; card stock; scissors; felt, pellon, flannel, sandpaper, or the loop side of hook-and-loop tape

Getting Ready: Mount the Brainy Bunch puppets (pages 315–318) on card stock, cut them out, and laminate them for durability. Then, attach small pieces of felt or other material to the backs the characters.

Directions: As you read "The Science Fair," place the appropriate Brainy Bunch flannel board piece on the flannel board. After students have heard the story, take a vote to see which water experiment students liked best. Tally the results on the board or create a simple bar graph. Does the class agree with the science-fair judges?

Visual Memory: Zoe's Rainbow Show

Need: shallow baking dish, water, small mirror, modeling clay, flashlight, white paper

Directions: Demonstrate to the class how Zoe made a rainbow. Fill the shallow baking dish half full of water. Put the mirror in the dish so that it slants back, resting against the side. Secure it in place with the modeling clay. Shine a flashlight on the part of the mirror that is under the water. Have a student hold a sheet of white paper above the light. Adjust the paper's position until a rainbow appears on it.

Language: Zoe's Rainbow

Directions: After watching the creation of a rainbow like Zoe's, hold a discussion.

1. Have you ever seen a rainbow in the sky? Have you ever seen a double rainbow?
2. What was the weather like when you saw the rainbow? *(sun shining through rain)*
3. What is needed to make a rainbow? *(water and light)*
4. What color is on the top of a rainbow's arc? *(red)* What color is on the bottom? *(violet)*

Follow-Up: Try making a rainbow by holding a prism in a shaft of sunlight to see an arc of colors. Or, on a sunny day, go outside and use a garden hose sprinkler to make a rainbow.

Outdoor Adventure: Rainbows and Puddles

Need: day with rain followed by sunshine, puddles

Directions: To introduce the water cycle activity (page 270), take an after-a-rain hike. Look for rainbows and puddles. Discuss how water collects in low areas and why the water eventually disappears. Have students guess how long it will take for the puddles to dry up and note each estimate. Check the puddles periodically, keeping notes as they disappear. Ask, "Do puddles in the shade disappear more quickly or more slowly than puddles in the sun? Why?"

Outdoor Adventure: Make a Rainbow

Need: sunny day, clear plastic cups, water, crayons, paper

Directions: Go outside and group students into pairs. Demonstrate with the following steps how to use a plastic cup of water to reflect colorful rainbow arcs. Then, let students experiment to discover and record with crayons the color arrangement of their own rainbow arcs.

Steps:
1. Fill the cup with water.
2. Place the cup so that sunlight shines through it. Cups may need to be positioned on a bench or held up so that the arcs of colors fall away from them.
3. Place a sheet of paper where the spectrum band falls.
4. Use crayons to draw and record the colors seen in the rainbow arcs.

Follow-Up: Discuss the order of colors seen in the rainbows arcs.

Listening Skills: Jada's Water-Glass Harp

Need: eight tall, thin, glass drinking glasses; bowl of water; turkey baster; two metal spoons

Directions: To demonstrate how Jada's harp worked, set up a glass harp with eight drinking glasses forming an instrument that spans an octave.

Steps:
1. Fill each glass with a set amount of water. (See the diagram below.)
2. Tap each glass gently with the spoon to play its note. Listen carefully.
3. Then, tune the pitch of each note with a turkey baster. To raise the pitch, remove water from the glass. To lower the pitch, squirt in more water. If you are not musical, ask someone who plays a musical instrument to help you do this.
4. Play the one-octave scale on the harp and ask students to sing along as you play the notes. You may teach them the names of the pitches "do, re, mi, fa, so, la, ti, do" or simply have them sing "la" on every note. Discuss the facts that there are eight notes in an octave and that the bottom and the top notes are the same.

Optional: Try playing the water-glass harp with friction. Wet an index finger and carefully rub the rims of the glasses. Try to play a simple melody with this method.

Follow-Up: See Name That Tune on page 269 for another water-glass harp activity.

Visual Memory: Yuuto's Mt. Fuji

Need: salt dough ingredients (6 cups flour, 2 cups salt, 4 tablespoons cooking oil, 2 cups water), 20-ounce plastic soda bottle, baking pan, warm water, red food coloring, liquid detergent, 2 tablespoons baking soda, 1 cup vinegar

Directions:
1. First make salt dough: Mix the flour, salt, cooking oil, and water in a large bowl. Work the ingredients with your hands until smooth and firm. Add more water if needed.
2. Stand the soda bottle in the baking pan. Mold the salt dough around the bottle. Make sure you do not cover up the bottle mouth or drop any dough into the bottle.
3. Pour warm water into the bottle until it is almost full. Add a few drops of red food coloring.
4. Put 6 drops of the liquid detergent into the bottle.
5. Add 2 tablespoons of baking soda.
6. Are you ready for the volcano to erupt? Slowly pour the vinegar into the bottle. Watch the "lava" flow!

Drama: Bubble Magic Show

Getting Ready: For all of the following bubble magic tricks, you will need bubble mixture and wands. To make the bubble mixture, combine 6 cups water and 2 cups dishwashing liquid. Stir it well, but do not shake it. Then, add 3/4 cup corn syrup and stir again. Store it in an airtight container.

Directions: Amaze your class with Eli's trick plus four more bubble tricks. Be sure to practice them in advance. Then, with great fanfare, demonstrate each trick. After each one, explain to students how the trick was done. Have each student choose one of the tricks, provide the needed supplies, and allow the class plenty of time to practice their tricks. Culminate the activity by inviting another class or parents to watch the bubble magic show.

Popping Bubbles

Need: bubble mixture, bubble wand, paper drinking straws, bowl of water

Directions: Without drawing attention to this step, dip one of the straws into the bowl of water. Then, use the bubble wand to blow a big bubble and poke the bubble with the wet straw. Give a student a dry straw and ask him to poke the bubble without breaking it. After demonstrating the trick several times, explain that dry objects pop bubbles but wet ones do not.

Disappearing Color

Need: bubble mixture, bubble wand, yellow and red poster paint

Directions: Add a small amount of both yellow and red poster paint to the bubble solution. Ask students what color the bubbles will be. They may guess "orange." In front of a white wall, blow some bubbles—regardless of the added paint, multicolored bubbles will result because all bubbles are multicolored. A bubble's surface acts like a prism and reflects the light that hits it. The thicker the bubble solution, the thicker the bubble wall and, therefore, the more intense the bubble's colors.

Pop Predictor

Need: bubble mixture, bubble wand

Directions: Tell students that you can predict when a bubble will pop. Blow a big bubble. Watch the top of the bubble closely. When a black ring begins to form on top and the bubble becomes colorless, announce that the bubble is about to pop. Give repeated demonstrations. Then, blow several bubbles and tell the class which bubble will pop first. Students will wonder how you can make such an accurate prediction. Explain that a bubble's wall becomes thinner just before it pops. Because less light is being reflected there are fewer colors and a black ring forms on top of the bubble. Blow more bubbles and invite students to look for the black rings and changes in the bubbles' colors to make their own predictions.

Frozen Bubbles

Need: bubble mixture, bubble wand, plastic plate, freezer

Directions: Ask students how long a bubble can last before it pops. List their guesses on the board. Then, announce that you can blow bubbles that will last an hour or even longer. They will probably wonder how you can do this. Show them by blowing bubbles onto a plastic plate and then quickly sliding the plate into a freezer compartment. Return in an hour to see if the bubbles are still there.

Square Bubbles?

Need: bubble mixture, bubble wand, scissors, pint-size milk or cream carton

Directions: Cut off both ends of the pint-size milk carton to create a bubble wand. Ask students what shape they think the bubble will be. Some may guess "square." Dip one end of the carton into the bubble solution and gently blow through it. Students may be surprised to see a round bubble form. Repeat. Then, explain that all bubbles are round no matter what shape the bubble maker or wand is. Bubbles always pull themselves into the shape that has the smallest surface area—which is a sphere.

Outdoor Adventure: Bubble Day!

Need: Award Certificate reproducible (page 212), bubble mixture, bubble wands

Directions: On a sunny—but not windy—day, take students outside to play with bubbles. Who can blow the most bubbles with one breath? Who can blow the biggest bubble? Whose bubble will last the longest? Award certificates for a variety of bubble categories such as biggest, most bubbles with one blow, longest lasting, highest flying, furthest traveling, etc.

Critical Thinking: Soda-Bottle Boat

Need: large plastic tub, water, 20-ounce plastic soda bottle with cap, toilet tissue, baking soda, vinegar, marbles or small rocks

Directions: Fill a large plastic tub with water. Gather students around you. Lay out four squares of toilet tissue and sprinkle about a tablespoon of baking soda on each. Spread the baking soda out evenly and roll the tissue squares up. Place the rolled up tissue squares into the soda bottle. Then, add a few marbles to the bottle to weigh it down slightly but make sure the bottle still floats. Fill the bottle a quarter of the way with vinegar and quickly put the cap on it with one twist. Immediately, set the bottle in the tub of water, loosen the cap, and watch the bottle boat zoom. Ask students why they think the soda-bottle boat moves in the water. (The chemical reaction that occurs when vinegar is added to baking soda propels the boat across the water.)

Critical Thinking: Floating Egg

Need: water, two clear glass bowls or drinking glasses, 2 eggs, salt, tablespoon

Directions: Begin the demonstration by filling both of the glass bowls half full of water. Carefully place an egg into the water in one bowl and watch it sink. Then, one tablespoon at a time, add salt to the water in the other bowl. Let students take turns adding salt and stirring the salt into the water until it dissolves. After several tablespoons of salt have been dissolved, put an egg into the water. Continue adding salt, carefully stirring the mixture, until the egg floats. Ask, "What happened?" After students give their ideas, explain that adding salt to water puts more molecules into it, which makes the water more dense. An egg is more dense than water with no salt, so the egg sank in the freshwater. Adding salt to the water made the water more dense than an egg, so the egg floated when enough salt had been added.

Story Recall: Make It Right

Directions: Tell students that you will make statements about the Brainies and their experiments. If students think a statement is true, they should give a thumbs-up. Thumbs-down means the statement is false. After each thumbs-down, ask students to change the statement to make it true.

1. None of the science experiments used water. *(False—all of the science experiments used water.)*
2. Zoe's rainbow experiment needed light and water. *(This statement is true.)*
3. Yuuto made bubble magic. *(False—Eli made bubble magic or Yuuto made a volcano.)*
4. Eli's bubble mixture "sizzled, boiled and hissed and popped." *(False—Yuuto's volcano "sizzled, boiled and hissed and popped.")*
5. Jada played music by striking water glasses with two forks. *(False—Jada played music by striking water glasses with two spoons.)*
6. When Eli poked a bubble with a stick, it popped. *(False—when Eli poked a bubble with a stick, it did not pop.)*
7. All of the students in the class entered the science fair. *(False—only four students in the class, the Brainies, entered the science fair.)*
8. Yuuto's Mt. Fuji won second place in the science fair. *(This statement is true.)*
9. Yuuto used a flashlight to make a colorful arc. *(False—Zoe used a flashlight to make a colorful arc.)*
10. Zoe wore a top hat when she demonstrated her rainbow arc. *(False—Eli wore a top hat when he demonstrated his bubble magic.)*

Directions for Reproducible Activity Pages

Visual Memory: Milk Rainbow—Page 283

Need: Milk Rainbow reproducible (page 283); crayons; red, blue, and yellow food coloring; one cup of whole milk; liquid detergent; clear, shallow bowl

Directions: Demonstrate how the primary colors mix with this science experiment. Gather students around the table where you are working. Pour the cup of milk into the bowl. Add three or four drops of blue food coloring to the milk near one edge of the bowl. Being careful not to move the bowl, add the same amounts of red and yellow food coloring, evenly spacing the colors around the edge of the bowl. Discuss that the food coloring is less dense than milk so it can sit on the surface of the milk without mixing. Next, squeeze a drop of liquid detergent into the center of the bowl. After careful observation, ask students to tell what they think happened. After everyone has had a chance to guess, explain that the drop of soap changed the milk's surface tension. The milk and the food coloring moved away from the soap. As the food coloring moved, the colors began to mix and to form new colors. You may wish to repeat the experiment as students use page 283 to record and color the different stages of the experiment.

Visual Memory: Color a Rainbow—Page 284

Need: Color a Rainbow reproducible (page 284), crayons

Directions: After completing the outdoor adventure Make a Rainbow (page 266), pass out page 284. Have students color the picture with the appropriate arrangement of bands of color. You may want to teach them a helpful mnemonic with this little riddle: Name the man who lives in the rainbow. Answer: Roy G. Biv (R—red, o—orange, y—yellow, G—green, B—blue, i—indigo, v—violet)

Music: Name That Tune—Page 285

Needed: Name That Tune reproducible (page 285), water-glass harp

Directions: Use the directions on page 285 to create a water-glass harp. Then, use the notation to demonstrate how to play three simple tunes: "Twinkle, Twinkle, Little Star," "Row, Row, Row Your Boat," and "Mary Had a Little Lamb." Invite students to try to name the tunes as you play them. Then, pass out page 285 for students to take home. Encourage them to make a water-glass harp at home and learn how to play these and other simple tunes.

Follow-Up: Back in class, allow time for students to demonstrate some other tunes they have learned to play.

Critical Thinking: Sink or Float?—Page 286

Need: Sink or Float? reproducible (page 286); plastic bowls of water; paper towels; a variety of small objects such as paper clips, pencils, crayons, sponges, marbles, plastic spoons, metal spoons, coins, rulers, grapes, etc.

Directions: Fill a bowl with water. Gather students around you. One at a time, hold up an object and ask students to vote whether they believe the object will sink or float. Then, demonstrate with the object. Next, divide students into small groups. Give each group a bowl of water and objects to test. Challenge students to make a paper clip float. After they have experimented a few minutes, demonstrate how it can be done. Tear off a piece of paper towel that is slightly larger than the paper clip. Place the piece of paper towel on top of the water. Carefully place the paper clip on the paper towel. Wait and watch. Finally, pass out page 286. Have students follow directions to record with illustrations whether the objects they test sink or float.

Follow-Up: Send a second worksheet home with each student. Encourage students to continue to experiment and record whether other objects found at home sink or float.

Directions for Reproducible Activity Pages, CONTINUED

Story Recall: Whose Recipe?—Page 287

Need: Whose Recipe? reproducible (page 287), scissors, glue sticks, crayons

Directions: Have students cut out the pictures at the bottom of the page on the dashed lines. Match the science project items and the Brainies by gluing the pictures in the appropriate boxes. Allow time for students to color the pictures.

Following Directions: The Water Cycle—Page 288

Need: The Water Cycle reproducible (page 288), pencils, crayons

Directions: Begin by telling students that the water we drink has been around a long, long time—as long as the earth. Say, "When dinosaurs waded through a stream, the water we swim in now was part of that stream. The same water keeps going around and around in what is called the water cycle. The water cycle has four parts. The four parts have big names." Print the names of the four parts of the water cycle on the board: *evaporation, condensation, precipitation*, and *collection*. Pass out page 288. Read the directions below for coloring the four parts of the water cycle. Allow students plenty of time to complete each part.

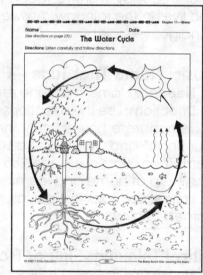

1. The sun heats up water in rivers or lakes or the ocean and turns it into water vapor. The water vapor leaves the river, lake, or ocean and rises up into the air. Ask, "Which part of the water cycle is this?" *(evaporation)* Have students color the evaporation part of the picture yellow.

2. As the water vapor rises in the air, it becomes cooler. Tiny drops of water begin to form. These become the clouds in the sky. "What do you think this part of the water cycle is called?" *(condensation)* Have students color the condensation part of the water cycle green.

3. When there is too much water in the clouds and they cannot hold it all, the clouds rain, hail, sleet, or snow. Ask, "What part of the water cycle do you think this is called?" *(precipitation)* Have students color the precipitation part of the water cycle blue.

4. When the water falls to earth, it might land in rivers, lakes, or the ocean. Or, it might fall on land. Then, the water either soaks into the earth and becomes part of the "groundwater" or runs off into a river or stream. Ask, "What part of the water cycle do you think this is called?" *(collection)* When the water collects in pools of water or soaks into the ground, the water cycle starts all over again. Have students color the collection part of the water cycle purple.

The Science Fair

Nearly every big kid
Was in the science fair.

But, just the Brainies in their class
Made something they could share.

The Brainy Bunch Kids—Learning the Basics

With a mirror in some water,
Paper, flashlight, too,

Zoe made a rainbow
Of yellow, green, and blue.

Bending light through water
And bouncing it below,

She won the fourth-place prize
For her color show.

Jada stood by glasses
With two silver spoons.

Busy hands a-dancing,
She played tune after tune.

Silver chimed on crystal
In B-flat and F-sharp.

She won the third-place prize
For her water harp.

The Brainy Bunch Kids—Learning the Basics

Yuuto's salt-dough mountain,
Was well prepared inside.

He poured in some vinegar
And quickly jumped aside.

KE-804011 © Key Education

The volcano sizzled,
Boiled and hissed and popped,

Spewing lava all about
When it blew its top.

The Brainy Bunch Kids—Learning the Basics

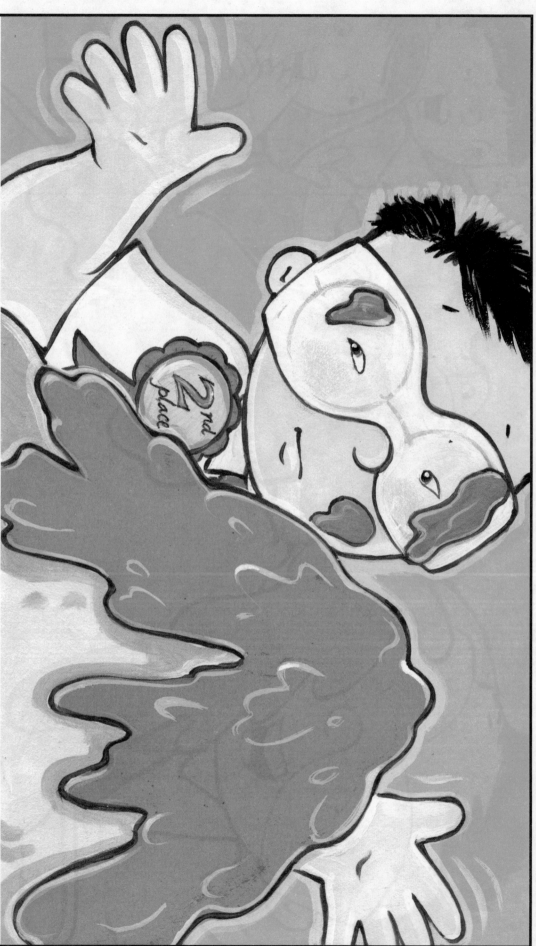

Yuuto came in second.
You could tell by his eyes

That he was disappointed.
He wanted the first-place prize.

He raised a wand up to his lips
And puffed his cheeks and blew.

Eli wore a black top hat
And stirred his magic brew.

Giant bubbles then were formed.
He poked each with a stick.

Then, something unexpected
Happened in this trick.

KE-804011 © Key Education

The audience was amazed:
The bubbles didn't burst!

And that is why the judges
Awarded Eli—FIRST.

Their teacher spoke with pride.
"History has been made.

The science prizes all were won
By students in our grade."

Name _____ **Date** _____

(See directions on page 269.) # Milk Rainbow

Directions: Draw and color the following four stages of the "Milk Rainbow" experiment.
1. Milk in the bowl
2. After three colors are added
3. After soap is added
4. After all of the colors have mixed

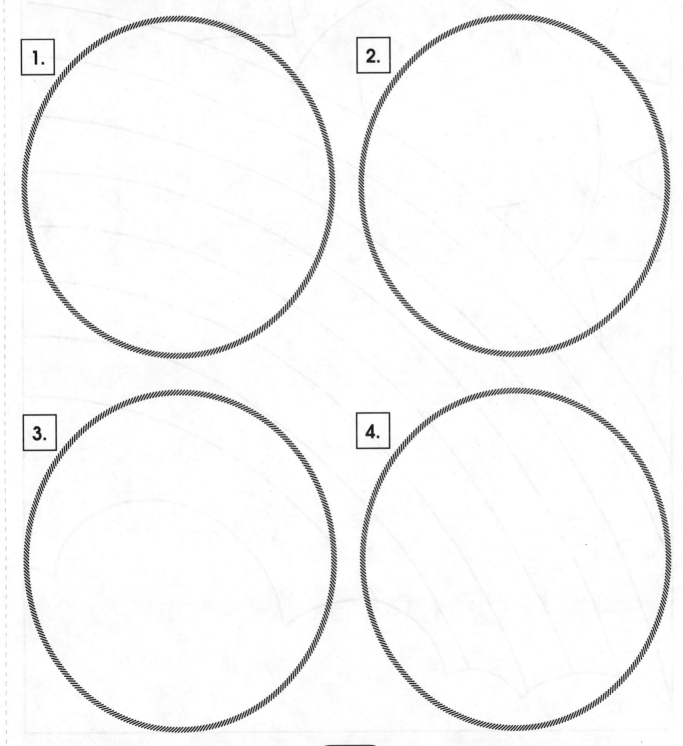

Name _____   **Date** _____

(See directions on pages 266 and 269.)

Color a Rainbow

Directions: Color the rainbow bands the correct colors.

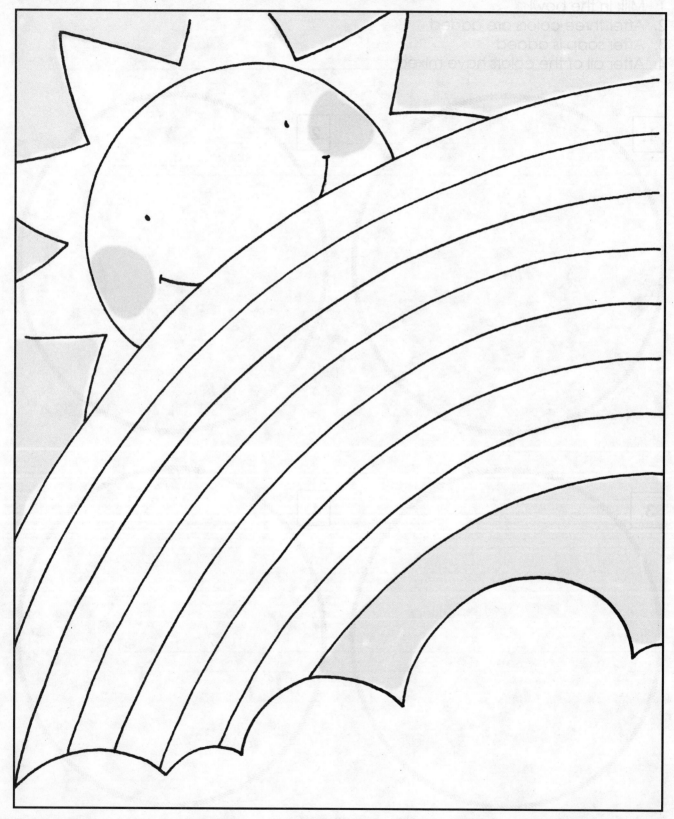

Name _____   **Date** _____

Name That Tune

Directions: Ask an adult to help you make and tune a water-glass harp.

You will need: eight tall, thin, glass drinking glasses; bowl of water; turkey baster; two metal spoons

Steps:

1. Fill each glass with a different amount of water. The first glass should have just a little water. The last glass should be almost full of water.
2. Tap each glass gently with a spoon to play its note. Listen carefully.
3. Then, tune the pitch of each note with a turkey baster. To raise the pitch, remove water from the glass. To lower the pitch, squirt in more water.
4. Use the water-glass harp to play the three tunes below.
5. Then, try to play other simple tunes on the water-glass harp.

Twinkle, Twinkle Little Star

1 1   5 5 6 6 5
Twinkle, twinkle little star,

 4 4 3 3   2   2 1
How I wonder what you are.

 5 5 4 4   3 3 2
Up above the world so high

 5 5 4   4 3 3 2
Like a diamond in the sky.

 1 1   5 5 6 6 5
Twinkle, twinkle little star,

 4 4 3 3   2   2 1
How I wonder what you are.

Row, Row, Row Your Boat

 1   1   1   2   3
Row, row, row your boat,

 3 2   3   4   5
Gently down the stream.

 8 8 8 5 5 5 3 3 3 1 1 1
Merrily, merrily, merrily, merrily,

 5 4 3 2   1
Life is but a dream.

Mary Had a Little Lamb

3 2   1 2 3 3   3   3 2   1 2 3 3   3
Mary had a little lamb,   Mary had a little lamb,

2 2   2   3 5   5   3 2   2   3 2 1
Little lamb, little lamb.   Its fleece was white as snow.

-285-   *The Brainy Bunch Kids—Learning the Basics*

Name _____   **Date** _____

(See directions on page 269.)   # Sink or Float?

Directions: On top of the water, draw the things that float. Under the water, draw the things that sink.

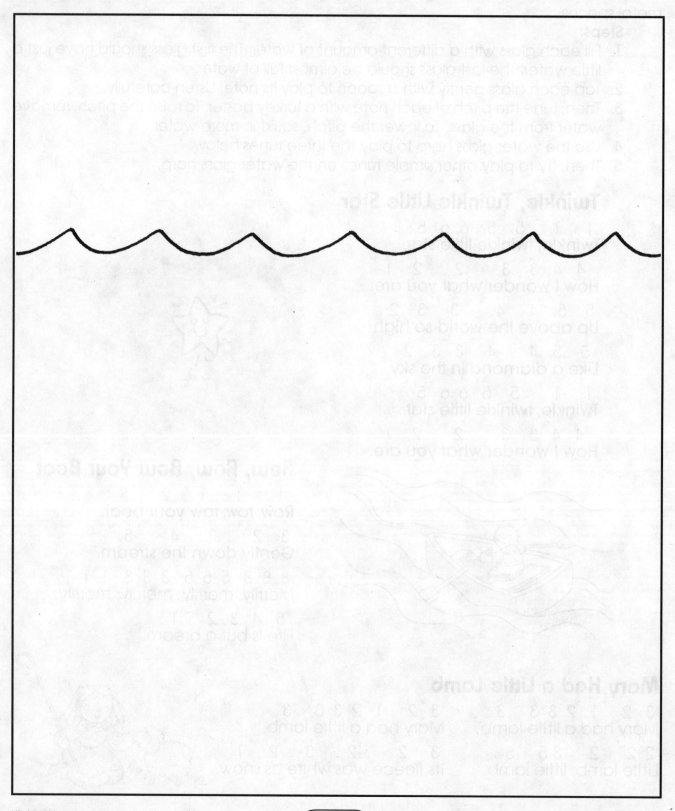

Name _____ **Date** _____

Whose Recipe?

Directions: Cut out the pictures below on the dashed lines. Match each set of science project items with its owner. Glue it in the correct box. Color the pictures.

Eli

Jada

Zoe

Yuuto

Name _____   **Date** _____

(See directions on page 270.) # The Water Cycle

Directions: Listen carefully and follow directions.

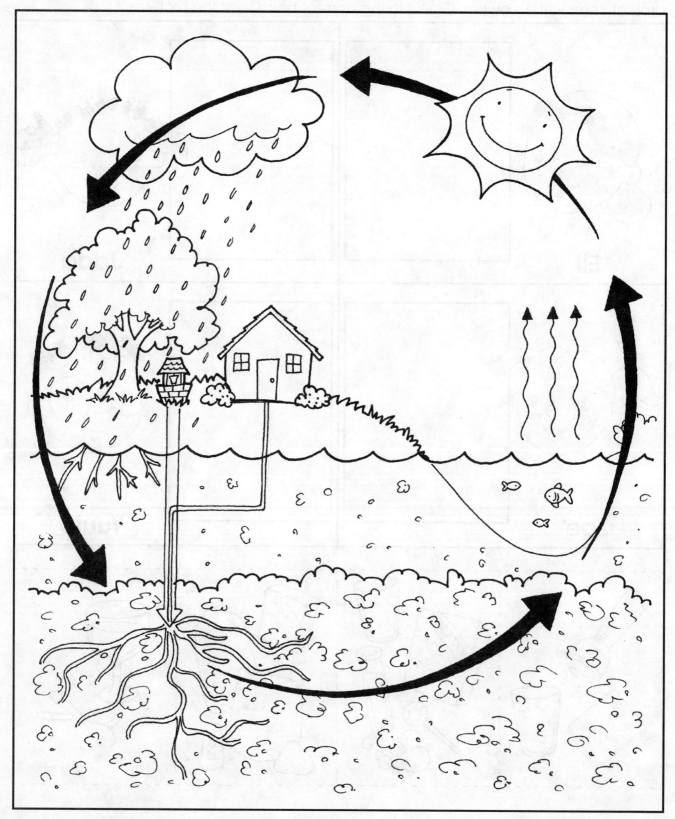

Chapter 12—Pets and Other Animals
(Teacher's Guide)

Learning Center: Setting the Stage for the Pullout Story "NO PETS ALLOWED!"
Need: shelves, small tables, wall area for displays
Directions: A learning center to celebrate pets might include the following:
- ❏ a scrapbook in which students may paste photos of their pets (page 292)
- ❏ pictures students draw of their pets
- ❏ books on pets and pet care and animal picture books and stories

Companion Book: *In the Small, Small Pond*
"Waddle, wade, geese parade. . . . Sweep, swoop, swallows scoop."
Need: *In the Small, Small Pond* by Denise Fleming (Henry Holt and Company)
Directions: Share the companion book. This 32-page book has only 64 words—each one rich and powerful! The page of dragonflies reads: "hover, shiver, wings quiver." And, those four words are enough. The boldly colored, simple illustrations look like vibrant paintings done by very young children; the art was created by pouring colored cotton pulp through hand-cut stencils.
Other Good Books to Share:
- ❏ *Hieronymus Betts and His Unusual Pets* by M.P. Robertson (Frances Lincoln Children's Books)
- ❏ *Pets* photography by Michael Dunning (Aladdin Books; "A Dorling Kindersley Book")
- ❏ *An Octopus Followed Me Home* by Dan Yaccarino (Viking)

Presenting the Pullout Story: "NO PETS ALLOWED!"
Need: No Pets Allowed!" story (pages 295–306)
Directions: Before reading the story aloud, tell students that they should listen carefully for the names of pets and other animals and remember as many as they can. Afterward, ask students to help you list on the board the pets and animals mentioned in the story. *(pups, parrot, cat, butterfly, beetles, crickets, spider, fly, fireflies, fish)*
Follow-Up: Challenge students to draw pictures of as many animals as they can remember hearing about in the story. Students may also refer to the list on the board.

Bulletin Board: Pet Parade Mural
Need: bulletin board; roll of white paper; black construction paper; 4" to 6" (10 cm to 15 cm) letter patterns; scissors; stapler or tape; pencils; markers, crayons, colored pencils, colored chalk, or paints; wide-tip black marker
Getting Ready: Cover a bulletin board or wall with yellow paper. Trace letter patterns on black paper and cut them out to make the title. Center the title at the top of the board.
Directions: Have students create a mural to celebrate pets. Begin by listing each student's name on the board. Beside the names, list the students' types of pets. If a student does not have a pet, suggest a virtual pet, a make-believe pet, or a toy stuffed animal. Divide students into small groups. Have students work in the groups to draw their own pets in pencil on the board. Then, invite students to color the animals their true colors. When all of the class pets have been drawn and colored, use a wide-tip black marker to print each pet's name.

Field Trip Ideas: Go See the Animals!

The following excursions will give students an opportunity to see and learn about a variety of pets.

❑ pet store
❑ your home or students' homes, especially if several different kinds of pets are owned
❑ animal shelter
❑ veterinarian's office

Craft: Paper Bag Animal Puppets

Need: animal picture books; lunch-sized paper bags; scissors; markers; crayons; glue; puppet decorations such as paper cutouts, yarn, fabric scraps, cotton balls, buttons, and ribbons

Getting Ready: Visit the library and have students look at pictures of their favorite animals. Discuss distinguishing features of each type of animal, such as noses, large ears, spots, etc.

Directions:

1. Give each student a paper bag. Demonstrate how to fold the bottom of the bag over to one side.
2. Have each student draw a mouth where the bottom of the bag meets the side of the bag.
3. Invite students to make their animals' distinguishing facial features by gluing the assorted decorations to their bags. They may also use crayons or markers to add colorful spots, stripes, fur, etc., to their animals.

Follow-Up: Let each student use the puppet to tell why that animal is a favorite.

Discussion: *March of the Penguins*

Directions: If you show only one video to your students this year, make it *March of the Penguins* directed by Luc Jacquet (Warner Home Video). The movie, a bit long for the very young, might be broken into several parts. Follow the showing of each part with a discussion.

1. Why do penguins walk so far? *(to get to their breeding grounds)*
2. Each year, how many eggs does a penguin lay? *(one)*
3. Who lays the egg—mother or father? *(mother)*
4. Who guards the egg—mother or father? *(father)*
5. Where does the father penguin keep the egg? *(on top of his feet)*
6. Why does the mother penguin leave after laying the egg? *(to find food to eat)*
7. Where do penguins get food? *(in the sea)*
8. How long does the father penguin hold the egg before it hatches? *(two months)*
9. How does the father penguin get food while holding the egg? *(He doesn't eat at all while holding the egg.)*
10. How old are penguins before they begin to lay eggs? *(about five years old)*

Following Directions: Ways They Move

Directions: Discuss with students the variety of ways that animals move. One at a time, give a movement direction while students move around the classroom in that particular way.

1. Lope like a llama.	11. Creep like a cat.	21. Spiral like a spider.
2. Trot like a tiger.	12. Prance like a pony.	22. Amble like an ape.
3. Glide like a gull.	13. Wiggle like a worm.	23. Waddle like a walrus.
4. Run like an reindeer.	14. Gallop like a gazelle.	24. Flitter like a flea.
5. Pose like a possum.	15. Frolic like a frog.	25. Peck like a peacock.
6. Leap like a leopard.	16. Flit around like a fly.	26. Scoot like a salamander.
7. Swim like a seal.	17. Buzz about like a bee.	27. Slide like a snail.
8. Skulk like a skunk.	18. Slither like a snake.	28. Stagger like a stegosaur.
9. Swoop like a swallow.	19. Crawl like a caterpillar.	29. Slouch like a sloth.
10. Tromp like a turtle.	20. Soar like a swan.	30. Scurry like a shrew.

Game: Guess the Animal

Directions: Tell students they will play an animal movement guessing game. Explain that the movement will always begin with the same sound as the mystery animal's name. (See Ways They Move page 290.) One at a time, call a student forward and whisper an animal and its way of moving in the student's ear. The student then moves like the animal while others try to guess the animal's name. As needed, give clues by naming the movements being performed.

Listening Skills: Favorite Pet

Directions: Have students sit in a circle. The first player says, "My favorite pet is . . ." and names it. The second player does the same and then repeats the first player's name and favorite pet, for example: My favorite pet is a cat and June's favorite pet is a turtle. The third player names her favorite pet and must remember the second and first players' favorite pets, too. Move around the circle adding to the list of favorite pets. When a player has difficulty remembering a classmate's favorite, that person may name it for him.

Critical Thinking: Name It

Directions: Gather students on the floor around you. Explain that you will give three clues about a variety of animals. When students think they know what animal you are describing, they should raise their hands. After giving all three clues for an animal, ask someone with a raised hand to name it.

Clue 1	Clue 2	Clue 3
1. is green	lives in water and on land	rhymes with *dog* (frog)
2. is tiny	lives on a dog	rhymes with *bee* (flea)
3. is a bird	has sharp claws	rhymes with *beagle* (eagle)
4. is very large	lives in water	rhymes with *quail* (whale)
5. is a bird	has colorful feathers	rhymes with *ferret* (parrot)
6. is tiny	makes honey	rhymes with *flea* (bee)
7. is small	looks like a mouse with wings	rhymes with *rat* (bat)
8. is a pet	likes to bark	rhymes with *hog* (dog)

Music: The Animal Fair

Directions: Write the lyrics on the board for the familiar song, "I Went to the Animal Fair." Teach students the song. Then, erase some of the animal names and descriptive words. Let students name new animals and descriptions and add them to the song. Sing each new version the class creates.

Original Version:
I went to the animal fair.
The birds and the beasts were there.
The big baboon by the light of the moon
Was combing his auburn hair.
The monkey bumped the skunk
And sat on the elephant's trunk;
The elephant sneezed and fell to his knees,
And that was the end of the monk,
The monk, the monk, the monk.

New Version:
I went to the animal fair.
The dogs and the cats were there.
The big raccoon by the light of the moon
Was combing his striped hair.
The honeybee bumped the flea
And sat on the centipede's knee;
The centipede sneezed and fell to his knees,
And that was the end of the bee,
The bee, the bee, the bee.

Game: Can You Hold It?

Directions: Tell students to listen as you name animals. If the animal is small enough to hold, they should give a thumbs-up. Showing a thumbs-down means the animal is too big to hold. After playing the game awhile, change the question to whether or not students would *like* to hold the animal.

Language: Class Pets Scrapbook

Need: a scrapbook with at least as many pages as number of students, glue sticks, fine-tip black markers

Directions: Ask students to bring in photographs of their pets. If photographs are not available, students may draw and color pictures of their pets. If a student does not have a pet, the student may choose to draw a virtual pet, make-believe pet, or toy stuffed animal. Give each student a page in the scrapbook on which to paste the pet photo and/or drawing. Help students print the names of their pets. When the scrapbook is complete, share it in large group.

Follow-Up: Place the scrapbook in the learning center.

Imagination: Three-in-One Animals

Directions: Invite students to lie back and relax. Instruct them to close their eyes and listen carefully to see with their imaginations the combinations of three animals you will describe. To give students time to use their visual memories and imaginations, pause at least 15 seconds after each description.

1. gir-phant-cock: giraffe with an elephant's trunk and a peacock's tail (pause)
2. bab-eh-roo: baboon with elephant ears and kangaroo's pouch (pause)
3. sna-key-ale: snake with donkey ears and whale's tail (pause)
4. sea-monk-eep: seal with a monkey's head and sheep's tail (pause)
5. gor-bill-pus: gorilla with a duck-billed platypus head and eight octopus legs (pause)
6. pan-ant-ma: panda with a big ant head and long llama legs (pause)
7. duh-pill-cow: duck with caterpillar head and cow legs (pause)
8. rab-urt-coon: rabbit with a turtle head and raccoon tail (pause)

Visual Memory: Illustrate Three-in-One Animals

Getting Ready: On the board, print the names of the eight three-in-one animals (see above).

Directions: Help students pick one of the creatures or invite them to make up original animal combinations of their own. Print each student's make-believe animal's name on a piece of drawing paper. Then, allow time for students to draw and color their three-in-one creatures.

Follow-Up: Play a guessing game. Hold up each picture and let students take turns guessing which three animals were combined to make the creature.

Outdoor Adventure: Show My Pet

Getting Ready: First, be sure to check your school district's policy regarding animals in the classroom. Then, send home a note to parents outlining plans for "Show My Pet" days and inviting parents to visit the classroom with their child's pet (all pets must be leashed or caged). Also, request information about possible allergies to animals or other concerns parents may have. Schedule separate times for each parent-and-pet visit. Invite children to ask questions about the pet, including how to care for it. Then, ask children to help you list each pet's attributes (see examples listed below) on chart paper. Take a photograph of the pet to attach to the list.

- ❑ quiet or loud
- ❑ one or two colors or many colors
- ❑ spots or stripes
- ❑ active or resting
- ❑ big or small

- ❑ long tail or short tail
- ❑ long ears or short ears
- ❑ soft fur or wiry fur
- ❑ shell or no shell
- ❑ feathers or no feathers

Follow-Up: Use the data collected about pets' attributes to make comparisons between specific categories. Tally and count totals, create "more and fewer" statements, and graph quantities. You may wish to fill out and present award certificates (page 212) recognizing the special characteristics of each pet.

Directions for Reproducible Activity Pages

Language: Pet Graph—Page 307

Need: Pet Graph reproducible (page 307), pencils, crayons

Directions: On the board, draw a grid similar to page 307. You may need more spaces than pictured since you will be recording information about the whole class. Have each student name a favorite pet. Use the initials of students' first and last names to record the information on the graph from bottom to top.

Follow-Up: Discuss the finished graph. What is the most popular kind of pet? Least popular? Then, pass out page 307. Explain that students should make a graph by collecting at least 10 sets of initials in the boxes, each student writing in the column above his favorite pet. When students have completed their graphs, meet as a large group to compare them.

1. Are the students' graph results similar to the graph created on the board? Are any graphs exactly alike?
2. Which pet seems to be the most popular? Least popular?
3. Why are some graphs very different? (Certain groups of friends may all like one type of animal better, etc.)

Bonus Activity: The grid reproducible may be used again to create a different graph. Have students use page 307 to record which of the pets classmates have actually owned. Compare the results of these graphs in large group, too.

Story Recall: Who?—Page 308

Need: Who? reproducible (page 308), pencils or crayons

Directions: Reread "NO PETS ALLOWED!" Pass out page 308 and read aloud each question as students follow along. Have students answer each question by circling the correct Brainy picture or pictures.

Follow-Up: After students have completed the worksheets, meet in large group. Again, read "NO PETS ALLOWED!" Have students raise their hands when they hear an answer to one of the questions. Then, discuss each question and its answer.

Outdoor Adventure: Creepy-Crawler Scavenger Hunt—Page 309

Need: Creepy-Crawler Scavenger Hunt reproducible (page 309), pencils, crayons

Directions: Divide students into pairs and give each pair a copy of page 309. Go to a park, playground, or nearby wooded area. Have students search the area to find and identify a few of the bugs or animals pictured on their sheets. Make sure students understand that they are only to observe the bugs or animals; they are not to pick them up or try to collect them. After a given time, meet as a group to see which creatures have been spotted in the area.

Follow-Up: Give each student another copy of page 309 to take home. With an adult's help, have students find pictures of the bugs or animals in books, picture dictionaries, or encyclopedias. Then, the student should choose several bugs or animals to draw and color the appropriate colors.

Critical Thinking: What's Wrong?—Page 310

Need: What's Wrong? reproducible (page 310), pencils, crayons

Directions: Pass out page 310. Begin by explaining that there are six mistakes in the picture. Students should find each mistake and circle it. Then, they may color the rest of the picture any colors they choose.

Follow-Up: After students have completed the worksheets, meet in a large group and take turns sharing ideas about how the mistakes shown in the picture could be corrected.

Story Recall: Illustrate the Story—Page 311

Need: Illustrate the Story reproducible (page 311), pencils, crayons

Directions: Pass out page 311. Read aloud the phrase in each box, repeating as needed. Allow plenty of time for students to illustrate each phrase.

Directions for Reproducible Activity Pages, CONTINUED

Critical Thinking: Wild or Tame?—Page 312

Need: Wild or Tame? reproducible (page 312), pencils, crayons

Directions: Pass out page 312 and explain the directions. Help students make decisions as they classify the pictured animals as wild or tame. Answers may vary.

Surprise Activity: Bugs Galore—Page 313

Need: Bugs Galore reproducible (page 313), scissors, glue sticks, pencils, crayons

Directions: Pass out page 313 and explain the directions. Help students read the names of the different types of bugs. Have each student pick four favorite bugs and cut out the names on the dashed lines. Then, students should paste each bug's name in a box and draw and color an example of each.

Critical Thinking: Which Does Not Belong?—Page 314

Need: Which Does Not Belong? reproducible (page 314), picture books about animals, animal pictures or posters, pencils

Directions: Discuss animal attributes using books and pictures for reference. Guide students to identify a variety of animal attributes, including the following:

- ❑ physical characteristics (Describe the animal's size, color, and number of legs or wings.)
- ❑ ways the animal moves (Does it fly, hop, run, or swim?)
- ❑ where the animal is found (Does it live on a farm, at a zoo, in a house, or in a jungle?)
- ❑ when the animal lived (Is the animal extinct or still living?)
- ❑ the type of animal (Is the animal an insect, bird, fish, or reptile?)

After discussion, pass out page 314. Explain that in each row, all of the animals—except for one—have something in common. Using the questions below, help students discover the animal attribute category in each row and decide which animal doesn't belong. Encourage creativity—students may point out other common attributes.

1. In the first row, how do all of the animals except one move? *(All can fly except the alligator.)* Cross out the animal that cannot fly. The others are all a certain kind of animal. What are they? *(birds)*
2. Except one, where might you see all of the animals in the second row? *(on a farm)* Cross out the animal that you probably would not find on a farm. *(elephant)*
3. Except for one, where do all of the animals in the third row live? *(in water)* Cross out the one that doesn't belong. *(butterfly)* What can all of the animals do that a butterfly can't? *(swim)* What can a butterfly do that the others cannot do? *(fly)*
4. In the fourth row, what do all but one of the animals have in common? *(They are dinosaurs.)* Which animal is not a dinosaur? *(bat)* Cross it out.
5. Except for one, the fifth row is all what kind of animal? *(bug)* Which one is not a bug? *(mouse)* Cross it out.
6. Except for one, where might you go to see all of the animals in the sixth row? *(the zoo)* Cross out the animal that isn't wild and would not live at a zoo. *(duck)*
7. In row seven, you might find all of these animals in a certain place. Where? *(They might be pets in homes.)* Cross out the animal that is not a pet. *(alligator)*
8. Row eight may be tricky. Except for one, all of the animals have a certain number of something. What is it? *(four legs)* Cross out the animal that doesn't fit the category of having four legs. *(spider)*

Chapter 12—
Pets and Other Animals

The Brainies got to thinking
Of something else to do,

But Zoe wasn't talking
For she was feeling blue.

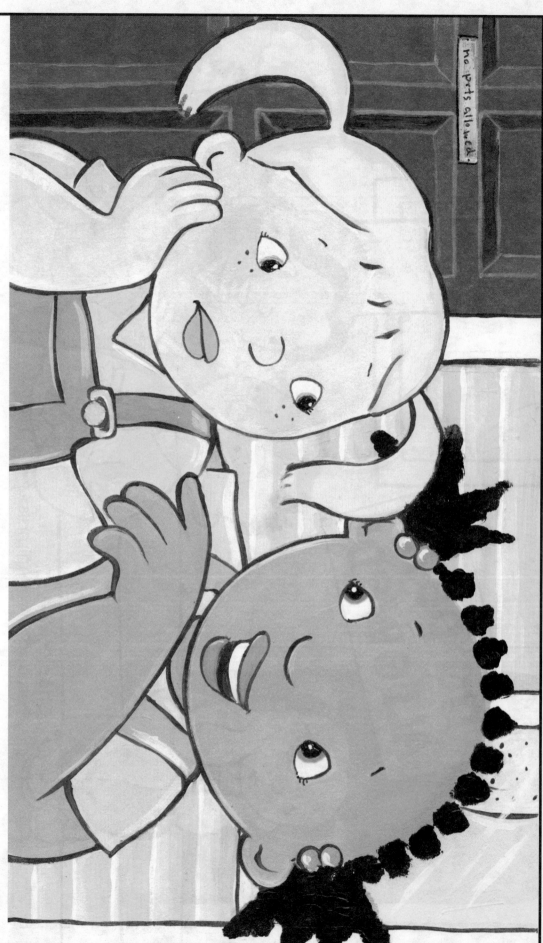

Jada said, "Now, Zoe,
Get your chin up off the floor.

I know that we can help you
'Cause that's what friends are for."

KE-804011 © Key Education

ABC·123·▲●■ ·ABC·123·▲●■ ·ABC·123·▲●■ ·ABC·123·▲●■ ·ABC·123·▲●■ ·ABC·123·▲●■ ·ABC·123·▲●■ ·ABC123·▲●■ ·ABC·123·▲●■ ·ABC·123·▲●■ ·ABC·123·▲●■ ·ABC·123·▲●■

Said Zoe, "Look at Eli.
He takes his pups for walks.

And you—you have a parrot
That screeches, squawks, and talks."

KE-804011 © Key Education

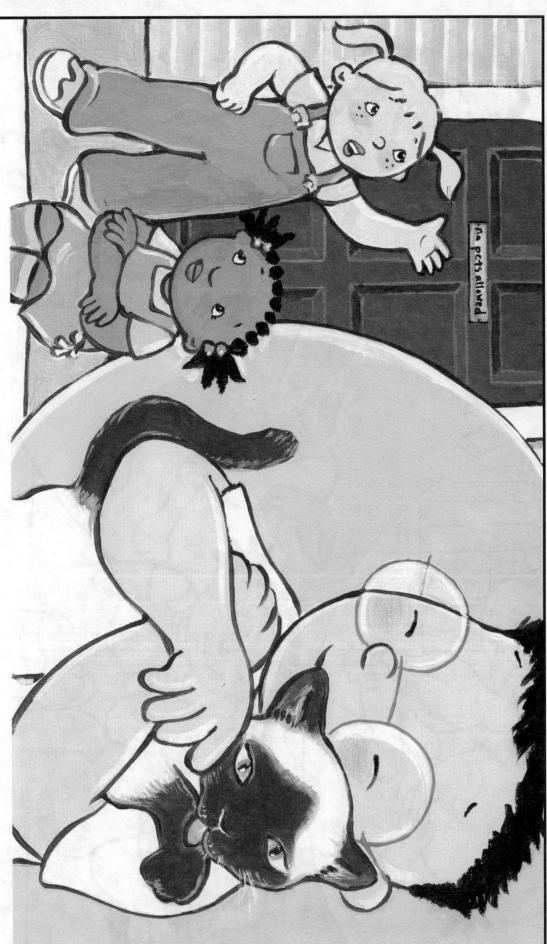

"Yuuto has his Siamese cat
That scratches, purrs, and meows.

But, the place where I live is
NO PETS ALLOWED!"

"I wish I had a little pet,"
Said Zoe to the three.

"Everyone I know has one,
Everyone, that is, but me."

So, they all got busy
'Til each one found a jar,

And to the park they scampered,
Which was not very far.

Zoe caught a butterfly
With stripes of green and blue.

Yuuto found three beetles
And six crickets, too.

KE-804011 © Key Education

The Brainy Bunch Kids—Learning the Basics

Eli trapped a spider
And a fly for it to eat.

Jada's fireflies glowed and winked,
Lighting up the street.

When Zoe's grandma found
What the kids had done,

She said, "Oh my! Mercy me!
I'll bet that you had fun."

KE-804011 © Key Education

The Brainy Bunch Kids—Learning the Basics

"But, bugs are not pets.
They will die, you know.

I think that it is time
For you to let them go."

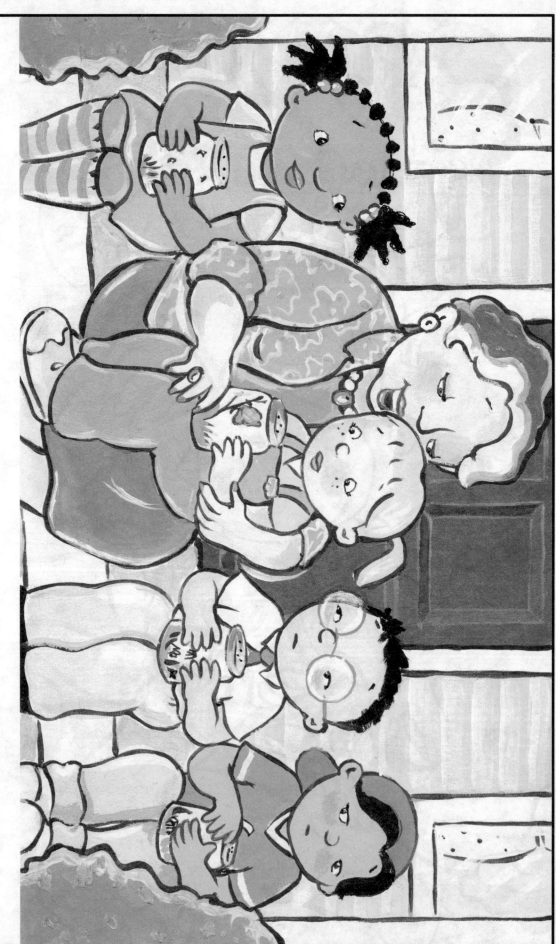

"Oh, Grandma, no!" Zoe cried.
But, what more could she say?

So, they took off every lid.
The bugs crawled and flew away.

"Don't you worry," Grandma said.
"Tomorrow, if you wish,

We'll walk down to the pet store
And buy my girl some fish."

Name _____ **Date** _____

Pet Graph

Directions: Look at the animal pictures below. Pick one you would most like to have for a pet. Write your initials in the square above it. Ask 10 friends to initial squares above their favorite pets. Then, color the squares that have initials.

Name _____ **Date** _____

Who?

Directions: Listen carefully. Then, circle the correct Brainy Bunch kid or kids.

| Eli | Zoe | Jada | Yuuto |

1. Who had pups?

2. Who had a parrot?

3. Who didn't have a pet?

4. Who had a cat?

5. Who went looking for a pet for Zoe?

6. Who found a fireflies?

7. Who caught a butterfly?

8. Who trapped a fly?

9. Who found some beetles?

10. Who trapped a spider?

11. Who was promised fish?

12. Who wanted to help Zoe?

Name _____ Date _____

Creepy-Crawler Scavenger Hunt

Directions: Look for these things that creep. When you find one, write an X in the box.

☐ ant

☐ bee

☐ beetle

☐ butterfly

☐ caterpillar

☐ centipede

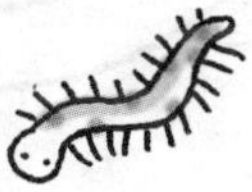

☐ dragonfly

☐ fly

☐ ladybug

☐ lizard

☐ moth

☐ snail

☐ snake

☐ spider

☐ wasp

☐ worm

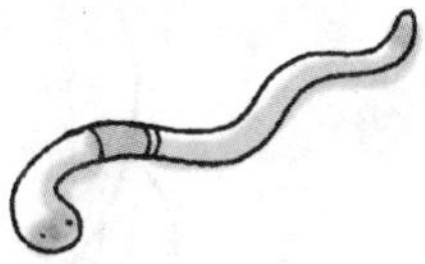

☐ other _____

☐ other _____

Name _____ **Date** _____

What's Wrong?

Directions: Find six things wrong in the picture. Circle them. Then, color the picture.

Name _____ **Date** _____

Illustrate the Story

Directions: Listen carefully. Then, draw and color a picture for the words in each box.

bugs crawling away	Jada's fireflies
Zoe's butterfly	Yuuto's cat
Eli trapping a spider	Eli's pups
Jada's parrot	Eli finding a fly

Name _____ **Date** _____

Wild or Tame?

Directions: Circle the wild animals in red. Circle the tame animals in blue. Then, color the animals any colors you choose.

Name _____ Date _____

Bugs Galore

Directions: Cut out the names of your four favorite bugs below. Glue each name in a box. Draw and color a picture of each bug.

beetle	caterpillar	cricket	daddy longlegs
dragonfly	earthworm	firefly	grasshopper
inchworm	ladybug	snail	spider

Name _____ **Date** _____

(See directions on page 294.)

Which Does Not Belong?

Directions: How are the animals in each row alike? Listen carefully. Then, cross out the animal in each row that does not belong.

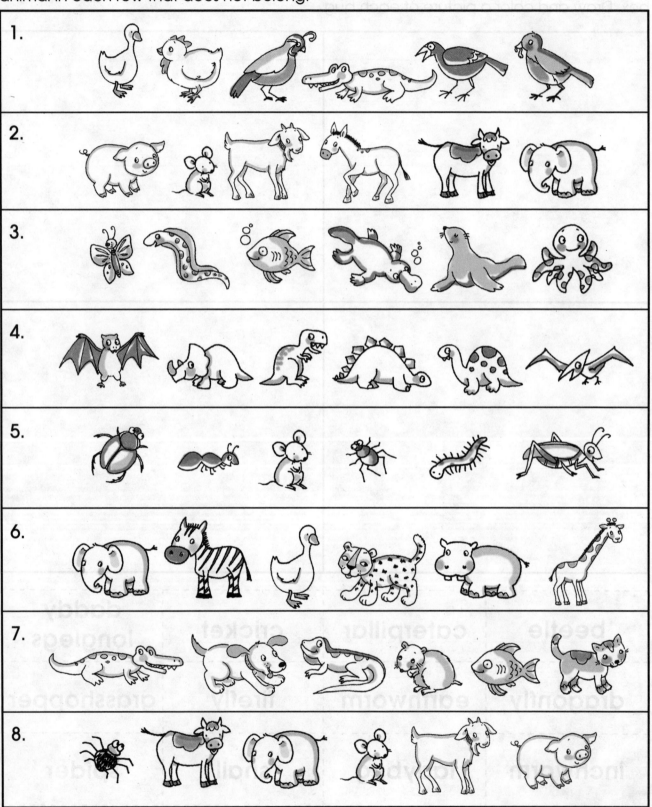

Brainy Bunch Puppet Patterns

*(See directions on
pages 6 and 265.)*

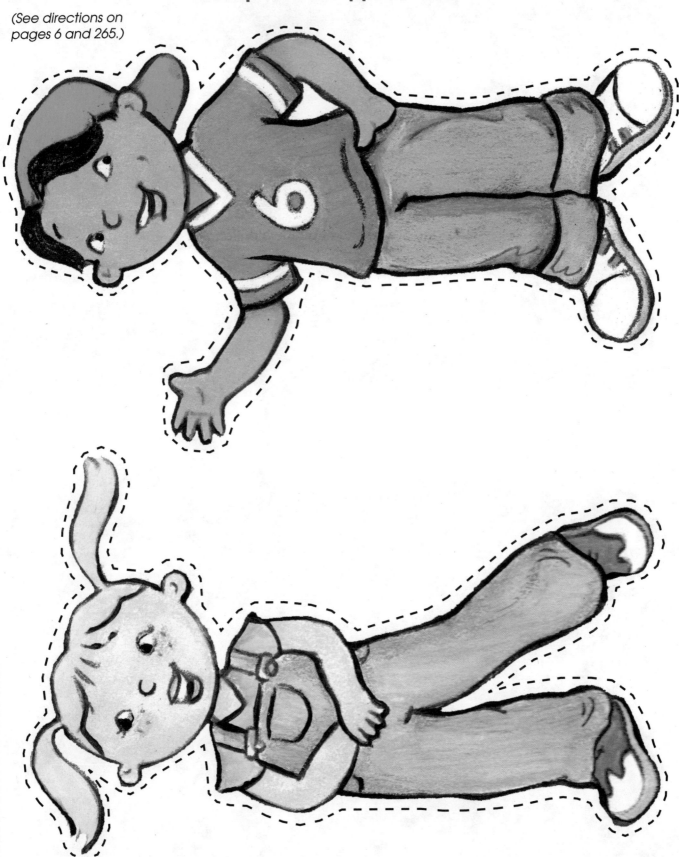

This page has been left blank intentionally.

Brainy Bunch Puppet Patterns

*(See directions on
pages 6 and 265.)*

This page has been left bank intentionally.

Answer Key

Page 27: Eli—baseball, soccer ball; Jada—book *Monster at My Door*, pen and paper; Zoe—jump rope, ballet slippers; Yuuto—sheet of music, violin

Page 28: The following missing things should be drawn in the bottom picture: 1. a star on the playground equipment; 2. a heart on the playground equipment; 3. Zoe's hopscotch rock; 4. the eye circle on the riding toy; 5. polka dots on Jada's ball; 6. stripes on Jada's socks; 7. number 6 on Eli's jersey; 8. the cloud in the sky; 9. the sun; 10. the flower in the swinging girl's hair; 11. Yuuto's glasses

Page 53: Answers will vary.

Page 55: 1. Eli (circled in blue); 2. Zoe (circled in red); 3. Jada (circled in purple); 4. Jada (circled in green); 5. Zoe (circled in pink); 6. Yuuto (circled in yellow); 7. Zoe (circled in pink); 8. Zoe (circled in orange); 9. Eli (circled in brown); 10. Yuuto; 11. all of the Brainies; 12. all of the Brainies

Page 77: A. 3 bunches of grapes; B. 5 strawberries; C. 11 bags of chips; D. 9 soufflés; E. 3 pieces of pie; F. 11 deviled eggs; G. 9 hot dogs; H. 5 chicken legs; I. 12 pieces of pizza; J. 6 ice cream cones

Page 81: 1. pizza; 2. hot dog; 3. bag of chips; 4. doughnut; 5. pancake; 6. soufflé; 7. deviled egg; 8. ice cream; 9. chicken leg; 9. pudding

Page 102: tomato—red; crackers—blue; grapefruit—red; carton of milk—blue; slice of pizza—yellow; slice of cake—yellow; cheese wedge—yellow; sandwich—blue; head of lettuce—red; pie—red; slice of watermelon—yellow; juice box—blue

Page 106: 1. Zoe; 2. Yuuto; 3. Eli and Yuuto; 4. Zoe; 5. Yuuto; 6. Jada; 7. Jada; 8. Eli; 9. Zoe and Jada; 10. Zoe; 11. Zoe, Jada, Yuuto, and Eli (melted snowball); 12. Zoe, Jada, Eli, and Yuuto

Page 127: dentist—dental pick and mirror; police officer—handcuffs; firefighter—fire hose; doctor—thermometer

Page 129: 1. Yuuto; 2. all of the Brainies; 3. Jada; 4. Eli; 5. Eli; 6. Jada; 7. Jada; 8. Zoe; 9. Zoe; 10. all of the Brainies; 11. Jada; 12. Yuuto

Page 153: 1. brown—mule; 2. black—sheep; 3. purple—snake; 4. yellow stripes—cat; 5. blue—mice; 6. green—duck; 7. red—hen; 8. blue spots—dog; 9. gray—goat; 10. pink with brown spots—pig

Page 154: 1. Zoe; 2. Zoe; 3. all of the Brainies; 4. Jada; 5. Eli; 6. Yuuto; 7. Eli; 8. Jada; 9. Zoe; 10. Eli; 11. Jada; 12. all of the Brainies

Page 157: Row 1: 3, 1, 2; Row 2: 2, 1, 3; Row 3: 2, 3, 1; Row 4: 3, 1, 2

Page 159: Row 1. blue hippo, blue skunk, blue duck; Row 2. red cow, red hen, red zebra; Row 3. orange elephant, yellow snail, red alligator; Row 4. red sheep, yellow bird, red butterfly; Row 5. red frog, red fox

Page 179: toad—t; worm—w; zebra—z; platypus—p; cat—c; ant—a; seal—s; iguana—i; fish—f; robin—r; dodo—d; quail—q

Page 180: first column 1–13: 2; 2; 3; 2; 1; 2; 2; 2; 2; 3; 1; 3; second column 14–26: 4; 3; 1; 2; 5; 3; 1; 1; 1; 1; 1; 1; 1; Robin won the name game with five letters.

Page 181: A. 5; B. 4; C. 1; D. 6; E. 3; F. 2; G. 9; H. 10; I. 8; J. 12; K. 7; L. 11

Page 182: Japanese beetle, cat, unicorn, otter, zebra, newt, platypus, hamster, iguana, seal, quail, robin, bat, vole, gopher, fish, ant, magpie, worm, toad, dodo, katydid, X-ray fish, yak

Answer Key, CONTINUED

Page 209: surprised—green; sad—blue; angry—red; happy—pink; afraid—purple; worried—yellow; confused—brown; proud—favorite color

Page 231: red—Stop; yellow—Slow, Then Stop!; green—Go

Page 232: The following should be circled. 1. jet with bird wings; 2. rocket lifting off from the school's roof; 3. bus with a satellite dish; 4. semi truck with no back wheels; 5. vehicle with square wheels; 6. biker riding with no helmet; 7. fire engine carrying zoo animals; 8. child crossing the street between cars

Page 233: 1. jet (circled in red); 2. rocket (circled in blue); 3. ambulance (circled in purple); 4. freighter (circled in yellow); 5. fire engine (boxed in red) 6. car (circled in green); 7. train (boxed in orange); 8. semi (circled in pink)

Page 259: Students' drawings should show the cat and kittens in the barn's hayloft, hens on nests in pens, piglets in mud, a dog under a tree, ducks near a truck, a snake beneath a log, sheep grazing on a hill, baby mice in a corn crib, a goat eating poison oak, and a mule in a swimming hole.

Page 260: farm animals circled in red—cow, pig, hen, mule, duck, sheep, goat; zoo animals circled in blue—lion, camel, giraffe, elephant, hippopotamus, leopard, zebra; Drawings will vary.

Page 287: Eli—detergent, water, corn syrup, bubble wand; Jada—water glass, spoons; Zoe—flashlight, mirror, water; Yuuto—baking soda, salt, flour, soda bottle

Page 308: 1. Eli; 2. Jada; 3. Zoe; 4. Yuuto; 5. all of the Brainies; 6. Jada; 7. Zoe; 8. Eli; 9. Yuuto; 10. Eli; 11. Zoe; 12. Eli, Jada, and Yuuto

Page 310: The following should be circled. 1. animal with a cat's body and tail and a rabbit's head; 2. Jada's ice skates; 3. whale in the lake; 4. dinosaur in the trees; 5. fish flying with wings; 6. Zoe's shoe and bare foot

Page 312: Answers may vary. Wild animals circled in red—elephant, alligator, giraffe, leopard, lion, hippopotamus, zebra; Tame animals circled in blue—chicken, sheep, cow, pig, mule, duck, dog, cat, goat

Page 314: 1. alligator; 2. elephant; 3. butterfly; 4. bat; 5. mouse; 6. duck; 7. alligator; 8. spider